What They Are Saying About *Notes From The Trail*

"*David Barol's account is packed with humorous and astute observations about the Appalachian Trail and the wonders of this beautiful planet. If you liked Bill Bryson's* A Walk in the Woods, *you'll love David's prose!*"

– Ben Feldman, Author

"*I thoroughly enjoyed this Trip along "Your Trail"*"
– Marcia Hineline, Park Ranger

"*…brings the humor of the Catskills to the gritty reality of the Appalachian Trail*"

– Leah Hoffman, Anthropologist

"*…makes me better appreciate the generation who worked so hard to make this a high-integrity, productive nation.*"

– Andrea Trulson Dolph, Author

"*Read the book in two days on the beach. Loved it.*"
– Mark Booz, Attorney

"*This is an extremely engaging account of a young man's adventures on the Appalachian Trail in a time that seems long ago (the mid-1970s). The real focus of the book, though, isn't the trials, tribulations, and rewards of hiking the AT, but … of what happens when we try to follow someone else's dreams rather than our own.*"

– Scott Nance, International Attorney

"*The book has thoughtful elements that reminded me of* Zen and the Art of Motorcycle Maintenance, *in its consideration of quality, although the story is much lighter, betraying a youthful playfulness in the author simultaneously serious and lighthearted like jazz.*"

– Intellectual Wanderer

Notes From The Trail
Book Two

The
Glorious
Quest

David Barol

Bala House Publishing
Bala Cynwyd

For information about permission to
reproduce selections from this book, write to:
Permissions, Bala House Publishing
Info@BalaHouse.com

For information about special discounts
for bulk purchases, please contact:
Bala House Special Sales at Info@BalaHouse.com

Manufacturing by CreateSpace.

Cover art by Judith Morris
Illustrations by Jada Byrd and Galen McMullen
Book design by Deborah Bradseth, Tugboat Design

Library of Congress Cataloging-in-Publication Data
Barol, David 1957-

Notes From The Trail: The Glorious Quest / David Barol.

ISBN 978-0-9914559-2-8

To my wife and family who stuck by me

You shall not steal; neither shall you deal falsely, nor lie one to another. You shall not profane the name of God: I am the LORD.

You shall not oppress your neighbor, nor rob him; you shall not withhold the wages of a hired servant overnight. You shall not curse the deaf, nor put a stumbling-block before the blind, but you shall fear thy God: I am the LORD.

You shall live justly; you shall not favor the poor because they are poor, nor the rich because they are rich; but in all things, deal justly.

– Leviticus 19: 10-15

CONTENTS

ILLUSTRATIONS

Cover: The Glorious Quest – *J. Morris*

Map of the Appalachian Trail – *J. Byrd*

August 12. "Now, that's a fly." – *G. McMullen*

August 13. "Safe at Hawk Mountain." – *G. McMullen*

August 18. "On the Parkway, at last." – *J. Byrd*

August 18. "If not now, when." – *J. Barol*

August 19. "Why a duck?" – *J. Byrd*

August 27. "Saved by the berry." – *G. McMullen*

August 30. "Gotta fetch." – *J. Barol*

August 30. "The fox trot." – *J. Byrd*

August 30. "The ever-loving Keezle." – *J. Byrd*

September 9. "The University." – *G. McMullen*

September 13. "Want an apple, deer?" – *G. McMullen*

September 13. "Revenge of the attack squirrel." – *G. McMullen*

WARNING!!

This is the story of a young man who finds himself walking the Appalachian Trail; he didn't go forth in life to hike the Trail, but there he found himself, slogging away. He started in Maine with the goal of walking two thousand miles to Georgia. By the time we pick up the story in *The Glorious Quest*, he has suffered cold and rain, hunger and thirst, loneliness and desperation.

And yet, this is not a book on backpacking. Back when the story takes place, in the Seventies, the number of people known to have hiked the whole Trail totaled about seventy. Nowadays, it seems everyone and her brother has hiked the Appalachian Trail. But back then this was an unusual way to spend the summer.

Remember Book One, *The Long Green Tunnel*? Why it was practically a guidebook on how to ruin a relationship. The two friends were clever in loading a pack, but not so clever when it came to sharing their vision. Broken packs they could fix, but they could never figure out how to repair their friendship. They witnessed the same beautiful vistas, but never figured out how to share their dreams. Like many partnerships, what started off with the flame of passion soon turned to smoldering resentment. That was the purpose in Book One. For *The Glorious Quest*, I hope this helps you find the courage to go after what you are looking for.

The events that take place in *Notes from the Trail* took place in real life. The people are real. Their names are real too. Only the names of the dogs have been changed to respect their privacy.

So, tie up your boots and heft your pack, as if you too are setting off on a long journey. You may as well be, for, as Robert Pirsig said in *Zen and the Art of Motorcycle Maintenance*, "*The journey you take is of yourself.*"

– DAVID BAROL

Notes From The Trail
Book Two

The Glorious Quest

CHAPTER ONE

Belief

AUGUST 12.

Hawk Mountain

> *"Gi'me a ticket for an aeroplane. Ain't got time
> to take a fast train. Lonely days are gone; I'm a
> going home; My Baby, done wrote me a letter."*
> – Joe Cocker

Even though I knew only this one verse to the song, I sang it over and over as I dashed through New Jersey and Pennsylvania on my way to one rendezvous after another. My goal is to plant my flag atop Springer Mountain in Georgia, still a thousand miles from the mountain top where I sit now, writing in my journal as I await the ride that will take me for my brief visit home.

The last few days have flashed by as I raced down the Trail. I wake at dawn and walk until dark, leaving little time for writing or reading. I averaged about ten miles a day when I started the Trail in Maine. Now, I am averaging over twenty miles each day, and on occasion, hiking more than thirty.

This does not leave much time to smell the flowers.

I arrived here at Hawk Mountain, Pennsylvania, after two days that would convince any sane person to accept a ride home – and stay there.

Because the rain was pouring when I climbed out of Wind Gap two days ago, I was wearing my poncho. But climbing up the steep slope made me sweat so much I was wetter wearing the poncho than without it. So, I packed it away, along with my shirt, taking advantage of the free shower. Walking in the rain no longer fazed me, not after Maine.

As I walked along the tree covered ridge, a lone horsefly circled my legs, occasionally bumping me. A horsefly is too big and clumsy to alight on a pair of moving legs. But its tactics of bumping me, plus the threat of its painful bite, made it a nuisance. I walked faster, hoping I could lose it. But as I sped up, more flies joined the chase. Soon I was enveloped in a cloud of long, gray flies circling my legs, bumping me, hitting me, each trying to bite me. I walked faster on the rock-strewn path, but the faster I walked, the more they came, and the more frenzied they attacked. When I swung at them, they attacked with still more fury: first in tens, then in hundreds. I ran. More joined the attack, zipping at me, smacking my legs, filling the woods with their hideous buzzing. I stopped, slapping any so stupid as to land on me. One bit me on the back of my thigh, but after a few seconds, the odious creatures disappeared. I looked around, but not one ugly, oversized fly remained, except for those lying dead on the ground.

Even though it was still the afternoon, standing under the trees, with storm clouds darkening the sky, it might as well

  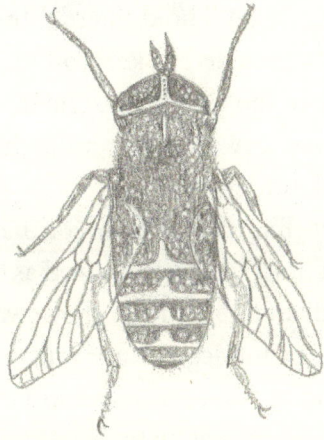

BLACK FLY   COMMON FLY   HORSE FLY

have been night. I began to walk, tentatively, first one step, then another. But just as before, a single, maladroit fly bumped my legs. First one, then another – then more and more. I ran, again attracting swarms of attacking flies. I stopped to beat them away. Again, they dispersed.

Only one bit me thus far, but their attack on my legs unnerved me. I do not like to kill living things, and the disproportionality of the many deaths I caused to the one bite I received, shook my sensibilities. Would it be fairer for me to limit my kills to each fly that bit me? Who is to say one bite is equal to the life of a fly? Maybe I should let two bite me for each one I kill?

"Do not attack me and I will not kill you." I hoped they understood English as it is the only language I know.

I put on my nylon rain chaps. Perhaps they would stop attacking me if they could no longer get through. As Yogi Berra said, "A good defense beats a good offense – and vice versa." If they stopped attacking me, I could live and let live.

"That'll hold them," I thought.

I needed to keep hiking. I was miles short of my destination: the George W. Outerbridge Shelter. From there, I hoped to hike twenty-four miles the next day, to get close to the Hawk Mountain side trail.

But flies care not for the plans of men. The chaps helped – at first. I scarcely noticed as the flies thumped against my nylon covered legs. Then they swarmed higher and higher, moving from my legs to my waist, my chest – to my head. This was too much; I ran as fast as I could over the rocky trail, swinging my arms wildly to prevent them from attacking my face. I was afraid they would bite my eyes. One got through my defenses and bit me on the back of my neck. I slapped – too late. Another bit me on my side and another on my back; I could not go on like this. They were forcing me to stop, but I was far short of the shelter – and if I did stop for the night, what was to say the flies would not return when I started the next day?

Another bit me, this time on my head. I slapped, then tripped on a rock, cutting my knee. I lay there, totally exposed to the flies, but they again dispersed. This made no sense. Did they attack with a purpose or was their purpose to attack? I crouched in a sea of sharp rocks without the space to sit. With so many miles to go, I dared not move, but I could not stay. I slowly stood, taking one step at a time, slapping dead any fly buzzing my way. I would kill them all if I must.

After walking a hundred yards, one tentative step at a time, I saw a clearing in the distance, where the power lines crossed the ridge. I remembered seeing this clearing near Route 33 on trips north to the Pocono Mountains.

I took a deep breath and dashed for safety. The flies attacked in full force. They landed and bit with their greatest intensity, as if trying to keep me from reaching the clearing. I stumbled on a rock. "Get up," I yelled. In two strides, ignoring the blood on my legs, I reached the clearing and dove head first into the damp grass. I slipped out of my pack and lay there, out of breath, letting the cool wet grass and the constant rain soothe the burning lumps covering my body.

I covered a disappointing twenty-four miles, falling short of my target by five miles. I stayed put, trying to put the horror I just faced out of my mind, with no assurance the nightmare would not continue the next day on the other side of the clearing.

Sometimes I wander through life aimlessly; other times, I believe each step is laden with meaning. There must be a reason for my life. As I lay there in the wet grass, I wondered what the flies were telling me. Since separating from my hiking partner, I no longer hike one step after another, being the hiker, but rather now I race from one destination to another. First, there was my race to put distance between me and Rand, my former hiking partner. Next, my race from Graymoor Monastery in New York to the Water Gap to meet Mark, my college buddy. Now, I am waiting on Hawk Mountain for my ride home to Philadelphia, after two days of battling flies, rain, and rocks. I am not the Zen hiker anymore; I am no longer "at one" with the Trail. I am someone holding my breath between wind sprints.

Why am I hiking the Trail if all I do is race to get off the Trail? I don't know; maybe the flies were telling me something.

Over the past few months, and along the hundreds of miles I have hiked, I sat atop mountains, stared over valleys, and watched the sunlight glisten off ponds. I stood in an almost religious awe under a cathedral of white pines at the Nature Conservancy in Maine. I fought mosquitoes and black flies, and sunk to my waist in mud. Despite it all, each day I put my pack on my shoulders to continue my journey as a thru-hiker on the Appalachian Trail.

During the race to the Water Gap to meet Mark, I did not sit by a pond, ponder a valley, listen to trees, or even chat with other people. Walking fifty miles in less than two days is a lonely business, and just because I wanted to get to my destination in time, there was no guarantee I would.

When I started this hike in Maine, not only was I hiking with a partner, I imagined I would meet people at every lean-to along the way or stroll with another human being along forest paths. I pictured there would always be someone to walk with during the day and to sit around a campfire, strumming a guitar, telling stories – and, who knows, maybe making love. I even bought a sleeping bag with a left-handed zipper which could connect to another sleeping bag with a standard zipper. But that didn't happen. With my luck, she would have had a left-handed zipper too.

Within the first few days after leaving Mt. Katahdin, we passed all the hikers who left before us. The weather in Maine before Memorial Day is too cold and the storms too harsh for anyone to begin to hike south from there and the unforgiving terrain turns the bad weather dangerous. Most of the earlier hikers quit the Trail within the first week; those we passed were nursing wounds from descending the relatively small mountain, Chairback. Hikers from the south easily climbed up the southern slope, then descended the rocky northern face. Those heading south, like me, learned how the strain of hiking down a long steep slope, with all the weight of the pack jamming the toes into the front of the boots, and knees straining to keep the body from falling forward, created so much pain that the only way to recover was not to hike. That is why we passed almost all the hikers who started before us over the next couple of days. My partner and I were able to survive this test: me, because I risked breaking my neck by leaping down the mountain and him, because more than any other human being, with the exception of Steve Jackson, was physically and mentally built to hike the Appalachian Trail.

Since that first day climbing Mt. Katahdin, I hiked each day alone. I shared a campsite most nights with my partner, but he became increasingly angry over having to negotiate each day's stopping points, whether a lean-to or a campsite. Then there was that night in Maine when he never reached our destination, the one day I stayed ahead of him. Normally, even when I left first, he would close the gap between us and then pass me without saying a word. But that one, miserable, rainy day, with its hordes of mosquitos attacking, swarming, enveloping, that was the day he never showed up. So, after a restless night, I went back to find his corpse, for that could be the only reason he would not have walked to our meeting place. Yet, disappointingly, I say now in retrospect, I found him nonchalantly stretching after a good night's rest in an abandoned fishing cabin. I thought he was dead, which would have at least left me with a better memory of him. Instead, he wanted to stop when he tired of walking, rather than walking to a destination we picked, sight unseen, out of the guidebook.

The way he imagined hiking the Trail would be to get up, hike, and then camp where he felt like it – by a stream, on a cliff, wherever his fancy found him. Instead, because he insisted we hike alone, he and I would have to negotiate a destination where we would meet each day. Negotiations and worry, planning and destinations – itineraries – were all things he hiked to put behind him. And here was me, the person he asked to hike the Trail with, needing to know where we would meet each day.

This was not what he dreamed about when he thought about hiking the Appalachian Trail. I never dreamt about hiking the Appalachian Trail, so what did I know?

After the night he did not show up, I began to wonder why he asked me to hike with him and I have increasingly questioned why I spontaneously accepted. I did not force myself upon him; he asked me to hike the Trail with him. In all the time since, he never once said he wanted to hike each day in solitude and maybe, sometimes, not even connect at night. Our visions of how this would turn out were so different that every other decision or issue paled by comparison. Does it matter who carries the peanut butter, when we cannot agree on whether we should walk together or even in sight of each other?

I occasionally meet people walking the Trail, although usually heading in the opposite direction. When I overtake someone hiking in my direction, they are out for a few days, enjoying the scenery, with no incentive to push to reach the high altitudes of North Carolina before winter hits. So, each day I walk alone, quickly.

Throughout the month of March, something like one hundred people left Georgia to hike north, in the opposite direction from me. Like ships passing in the night, I knew I would not hike with them, but I thought we would meet at the shelters and campsites along the way. In fact, I even made a date to meet a young woman, who advertised in the Appalachian Trail News for hiking partners. I replied, "Although I can't hike with you, as we will be hiking in opposite directions, perhaps we can meet for dinner sometime in July. I'll wear something blue." But I never saw her. I crossed paths with the last of the Northbounders back in New York; now, like migrating geese, they have all flown past me.

There is no sense of superiority separating a Southbounder from a Northbounder, although I think it must be easier hiking North than South, or why would there be so many more people traveling in that direction? I felt joy bumping into a Northbounder whenever we did meet and I knew some of them in advance from reading the trail logs or hearing about them from faster hikers.

The one superpower I want is the ability to reset my life, or at least live in two dimensions at the same, allowing me to select the best course of action. If I could reset this hike, I would leave from Georgia in March and finish in Maine in mid-summer. Starting in June in Maine was cold and wet: the state was not yet open for business. Of course, if it were up to me, I would have taken a semester in England, instead of walking two thousand miles. This hiking business was never my dream – it was Rand's dream – and his course load prevented him – us – from leaving in March. So, everything I did was because of my partner, whose red pack I will never see in front of me again.

I passed the most famous of the Northbounders in Bear Mountain State Park. They were the Snail Sisters, about whom I heard from every Northbounder. They were the first to leave Springer Mountain, but walked so slowly, every other Northbounder passed them. The first Northbounder we met, Andy Carter, no relation to the President, was the first to tell us about them and every other Northbounder I met asked me to send regards to them. Since I spent so many hours by myself, I must admit I fantasized about the night we three would spend together, but we met crossing a small brook, mid-afternoon, with nothing more than an intense chat and a fond farewell. I was of interest to them only because I was the first South-bounder they met, so I did not appear in their fantasies. I watched them walk away, knowing I would never see them, or any other thru-hiker, again.

My ex-partner walks somewhere behind me, maybe a day, maybe a mile back. The only reason we waited to end our partnership in Connecticut was because we lacked the nerve to end it during that first week in Maine. On the first day of the journey, my partner made it clear he wanted the walking part of the trip to be a solitary event, when at the first interesting thing to see, he said, "I hope you don't intend to stop every time I stop."

We experienced a cold, smoldering demise to our friendship. When we finally agreed to part ways, I left to hike south, while he reorganized his gear for the rest of his trip alone. The small stove I brought proved more valuable than the tent he carried, especially once we left that swamp they call Maine. He hitched to a bigger town to mail his tent home and to purchase a pack stove for himself. I quickly left Connecticut and headed south. I dread bumping into him on this long and narrow path. Of course, as gentlemen, we would conduct ourselves with a strained courtesy, then sleep that night with one eye open. So, I hurried off alone and will most likely stay this way for the remainder of my trek to Georgia.

When I awoke after my first night in New Jersey on August 7, I quietly packed my bag, taking care not to wake the weekend hikers, whom, like me, avoided the night's rain by sleeping on someone's porch in Unionville. The lights were out when I arrived and they did not come back on when I left; perhaps, no one was at home. Thanks, someone. After ten minutes of walking through the morning mist, I saw a sign pointing north – I thought the scenery looked familiar, in a backward sort of way. I turned around and headed south.

It was still dark when I left Unionville for the second time. I will always look back at the town with ambivalence. On the one hand, the half dozen letters waiting for me at the post office gave it a touch of home. But as stupidity would have it, in my haste to get to the post office before it closed, I made a deal with the devil and was punished for it.

I walked through a residential area, past a house with six people holding a cookout on the front lawn. One of them asked me for some tales of the Trail, which, of course, I obliged with the old standby about man versus moose. I told them about the plaque on Mt. Washington listing the many people who died there. How many others died along the Trail, I don't know. I know people died climbing Katahdin, and people drowned crossing the Kennebunk River. My audience didn't seem to care much for accuracy, just the gore.

I re-entered reality and asked for the time – it was past 4:30. My agitation was clearly visible, as I realized I would not reach the Unionville Post Office before it closed Saturday and it would not reopen until Monday. With the goal of meeting Mark on Monday, I could not afford to wait around. So, this man and his young son volunteered to drive me the five miles to the Unionville post office, wait by their car while I retrieved my mail, and drive me back to the exact spot I left the Trail. That is a big deal to me – hiking every step of the 2100 miles of the Trail. Since hiking the Trail was not my idea to begin with, what is the point of me hiking any of it if I start skipping sections? Up to this point, I have hiked every step of the Trail, except for the short-cut out of Maine, but at least I did walk out of Maine, albeit on a different, unofficial, path. And then there was the seventeen-mile section I missed after Rand and I hitched – separately – to the town where we split our possessions, but my not going back to where we left the Trail was due to my desire to put some distance between us. I have no way of knowing whether he went back to that lean-to where we spent the hour ripping into each other.

This was the first time I turned away a driver who would take me back to the spot where I left the Trail. It was not just the letters that kept me anchored; for there to be any chance of reaching the Water Gap in time, I needed to spend Saturday night in Unionville. I took my pack out of the car and sent them off. When I looked at their faces, my betrayal reflected back, and I felt like a skunk. What I did not see, was my walking stick, still laying in the trunk. When I looked around for it, it was too late.

When imagining my hike on the Appalachian Trail, my thoughts took me along forest paths and through alpine meadows. There has been lots of that. But the AT also crosses highways and runs along roads, sometimes for long stretches. The Trail extends over two thousand miles, a distance so long it leaves no time to frolic amongst the daisies; you either keep moving or give up hope of ever reaching the end. There is danger; there were probably a dozen times a slip here or a misstep there would have sent me to my death, but mostly there is monotony. Mile after mile, day after day – just walking; the trick to hiking 2,100 miles is to get up every day and hike.

Of course, near death experiences help to break the monotony. Many of my brushes with death were due to the physical and emotional toll that comes from starving. Losing my balance on a rock ledge would kill me. Being hoisted on the antlers of a crazed, teenage moose would certainly end the hike, but none of that happened. Maybe I hike as my penance for being just young enough to miss going to Viet Nam. Compared to spending the summer playing softball and tennis, the Trail is closer to the Nam experience, but no one has booby trapped my path and, although I may have secretly wished it, no sniper took out my hiking companion.

The first few miles south from Unionville took me along a highway, but once I stepped onto the dirt trail, my hand instinctively struck toward the dirt, but nothing happened. A walking stick is not just something to lean on. It has many other uses, such as propping up a pack, providing balance for crossing a log, or serving as a third leg when climbing a steep slippery slope, which was how I first happened upon it. When I walked on a dirt trail, I poked the stick ahead of me, walked past it, and then repeated. The walking stick created the pace, like the drum on a slave galley, an image I frequently pictured as I walked all day, every day.

I found the stick in Maine after I slid down the steep slope of Poplar Ridge; it accompanied me ever since. I thought about going back for it – I should have gone back for it – but I could not bear the thought of entering Unionville for what, in retrospect, would have been a fourth time.

By 9 AM, I reached High Point, New Jersey. For the first seven miles, I walked along asphalt roads. Of all the surfaces, asphalt is the worst. As Humphrey Bogart might have said, if he and Katherine Hepburn walked instead of taken a boat, "Asphalt. I hate asphalt."

Road walking forces the soles of the feet to absorb the

full impact of each step and causes them to land in the same position mile after flesh-mashing mile. I will never buy heavy leather boots again unless I go into construction. Each step presses the stiff, heavy leather against my toes and the tops of my feet. Road walking tests the difference between good socks and cheap socks. I started in Maine with great socks, but I sprinkled them, like bread crumbs, along the muddy trail, and now I am left with the cheap socks I bought from stores along the way.

To make matters worse, two miles south of Unionville, the mesh band near the top of my pack, the one responsible for keeping the metal frame off my shoulder blades, snapped. I was just minding my own business, not bothering anybody, and the darn thing ripped. A temporary repair with an ace bandage helped, but not by much – there was too much give. Instead of the mesh keeping the metal crossbars of the frame off my shoulders, the pack was free to sway with every step, digging a strawberry patch smack dab in the middle of my back. Not that I am one to complain – but I have not spent two days on this hike without dealing with some sort of blister, chafing, welts from bug bites, and now raw skin in the middle of my back. Yeah, this was how I envisioned the hike.

Back at school, where ten of us shared an old fraternity house called The Anchorage, one of our housemates offered to meet us at the Allentown Lean-to with supplies. Later, when his mom got involved, the plans grew into coming to their house for dinner and an overnight stay. But then her plans changed so she insisted I arrive three days earlier, which is why Mark met me at the Pennsylvania state line. As someone who understands the discipline of the Trail, Mark knew I needed to stay on the Trail as much as possible, but his mother was an irresistible force who wanted to help this poor wanderer, even if it killed me.

When I called from Graymoor Monastery, she told me her plans changed and she needed to attend a teacher's conference in State College. She suggested if I would just walk faster, I could reach the same lean-to three days earlier, hiking 150 miles in five days, rather than eight.

Let's do the math. Lots of people enjoy hiking. Three miles here, five miles there. But hiking twenty miles with a full pack over mountains is exhausting. If you do that on a Saturday, you may need Sunday to recover. I never in my life hiked twenty miles for two days in a row, carrying everything I owned on my back. Even as a boy scout, twenty miles was the limit and that was just carrying a canteen and a sandwich. Hiking thirty miles in a day, especially with the weight of the pack and the rugged terrain, would take more than a day to recover. Yet, if left to her designs, she would have me hike thirty miles a day for five days straight.

She offered all sorts of suggestions, such as throwing away some gear to lighten my load or getting up an hour earlier. She was full of help, a veritable encyclopedia of help. She forced me to come up with an alternative plan: Mark picks me up at the Delaware Water Gap, saving three days, but Mark drives farther from their house in Allentown.

The new plan still required averaging twenty miles a day for five days. I dawdled a bit that first day in Bear Mountain Park – even taking a swim – but for the rest of the time; I awoke at dawn and walked until dark. Now I know why the economists warn: "There is no such thing as a free lunch."

But come to think of it, I enjoyed several free lunches along the way. There was Thayer Hall at Dartmouth College, what we thru-hikers call the "Mecca of the Appalachian Trail." There was Mrs. Tufts, the "Mystery Woman," who brought thru-hikers out of the rain for home cooking, a shower, and a soft, dry bed. And there was Graymoor Monastery, where thru-hikers stop for gourmet meals, private rooms, and some good old ecumenical fun.

On the last full day of the mad dash to see Mark, I hiked thirty-seven miles south of Uniontown, hiking without pause, until long after nightfall. The Trail climbs to the top of the Kittatinny Mountain range, a level ridge without much change in elevation. The trail planners tried to make the walk interesting by weaving the path back and forth across a jeep road, but I caught onto their game and stuck to the dirt road. What did I see? Not much. The Delaware River flows some-where west and below the ridge, but I could not see it from where I walked.

Across the river, the land rises steeply to form another ridge, or rather, the Pocono Highlands. Not that long ago, the Army Corps of Engineers wanted the Appalachian Trail to skirt the shore of an enormous lake. The government seized farms and razed hamlets on both sides of the Delaware in preparation for building a dam just north of the Delaware Water Gap at Tocks Island. This would flood the land between the two elevations, providing hydropower and drinking water for New York City. It also would envelop a huge tract of land that people not only visited throughout the year, but also where they farmed and lived for centuries.

The Army Corps abandoned the project for geological reasons, but for many families, the plan drowned their lives. We used to visit friends from our neighborhood in Philadel-phia, who owned a farm house in Dingmans Ferry, on the

Pennsylvania side of the river, just north of the Dingmans Chase Bridge. The land belonged in their family for generations. They refused to leave, but because the government chased away their neighbors and destroyed the village of Dingmans Ferry, there was no one around to look after their place when they were in Philadelphia, where they worked and raised their family. Although they resisted, their house, often vandalized, their property, a haven for motorcycle gangs, no longer felt safe. Ultimately, they were forced to move, because of a dam that was never built.

I have fond memories of that house, with its big stone fireplace. There was also a barn, but animals no longer slept in it. There was an orchard, but by the time my family visited, it was halfway back to nature. A path led along a creek through the woods, winding past an old hunting cabin, to reach two crystal clear pools, fed by waterfalls. The only way to get to them was to walk. So many trout filled one of the pools you could reach down and pet them. The path to the waterfalls followed the narrow Adams Brook, filled with frogs and salamanders, which we used to catch with our hands.

How does one put a fair price on such beauty?

I am not suggesting anyone should care about this one family, when there were millions of New Yorkers who needed water. I should not weep for them; after all, look at how many people in Russia and Cuba lost their homes and property in the name of the public good.

I must have misunderstood those classes, but I thought the founders of our country warned us against a government that would take property for the public good, because once it establishes that power, it will take property for bad reasons as well. One of King David's sons, Ahab, took the land of a neighbor, not for the public good, but because his wife, Jezebel, nagged him to do it. Our founders wanted to prevent such governmental overreach.

When Mr. Jefferson, the founder of my university, who also served as the nation's third President, wrote The Declaration of Independence upstairs from what became a hamburger shop in Philadelphia, his original words were "Life, Liberty, and the Pursuit of Property." Near the final draft, someone altered the wording to "the Pursuit of Happiness." The founders knew that without the sanctity of private property, the government can deprive us of our happiness. Unlawful searches of our pockets and the unlawful seizures of our land both fall under those inalienable rights expressed in the first few lines of our Declaration of Independence.

There is something to be said for walking sixteen hours each a day to give a person something to think about. Because of a combination of low humidity and level ground, I walked until well after dark that first day through New Jersey. The moon lit the trail; all I needed was my tiny pocket flashlight to illuminate the spot where my foot would next land. At one of these steps, I froze with my leg in the air. There, in the faint beam of light, lay a five-foot rattlesnake. It did not bite me, as someone already beat it to death with a baseball bat or large rock. Still, I took it as an omen; my hike was at an end about fourteen miles north of the Water Gap.

I awoke the next morning, this time after dawn. Once I got past my typical morning pain threshold, I clipped along at a fast pace, stopping occasionally to munch some trail mix or to take small, measured swigs from my remaining water – there were no springs on top of this ridge in New Jersey. At noon, I saw the first sign I was nearing civilization: a pile of beer cans.

"How nice," I thought. "Bright green cans decoratively placed before a woodland setting." What I needed about then, walking under the August sun, was a full one.

Before long, I reached Sunfish Pond. Located between their two cities, New Yorkers and Philadelphians extol the pond for its outstanding purity. Nevertheless, with only five miles left until I reached the Gap, I dared not linger. Besides, the signs nailed to every tree prohibited lingering, along with any other type of activity. I looked around for a cop, then lingered long enough to taste the famous water. The warm, pond-tasting water let me down. I almost – almost – wished I were back in Maine. I desperately needed something to drink, but there was too much pond in this water.

Continuing along the bank, I spied three girls sunning themselves on the far shore – and they were not wearing any clothes. Times like these really tested my friendship with Mark. But I kept walking.

During the final few miles to the Delaware Water Gap, long out of water, feeling the heat on my body and the sticky feeling in my mouth, I observed I was in Genesee beer country from all the empties scattered on either side of the Trail. My father used to say, "Let it not be said, but said to your shame, that all was beauty until you came."

It was still before noon when I reached the parking lot at the Gap – fourteen miles completed before lunch. The Water Gap, where the Delaware River slices the mountain range in two is another of those sights of natural beauty, like Niagara Falls and the Grand Canyon, best stared at with slack-jawed awe. It is too wide for a photograph to fully capture the scene, not that I am carrying a camera. Despite the natural beauty, all I could think about was a cold beer to quench my overwhelming thirst.

Since I reached the parking lot at the Gap three hours before my rendezvous time, I planned to cross the river to find the Omega Health Food Store, my final link with the Snail Sisters and all the other Northbounders who recommended the whole-wheat pizza. But as I passed the first line of cars, I saw Mark reaching into the trunk of his car. He arrived early hoping to meet me along the Trail. When I told him about the sunbathers at Sunfish Pond, he said, "I am sorry I didn't get here sooner."

I handed him my pack, he handed me his cooler bag containing a six-pack of chilled Genesee beer.

Hey, a free lunch. Fifty-one miles suddenly became history.

AUGUST 13.

Another Free Lunch

Ever since splitting with Rand, I find myself enjoying the grizzliest of situations. There I was Sunday, fifty-some miles from the Water Gap. Undaunted by storms, a broken pack band, and sores on my ass, I reached the Gap with time to spare. And yet, through it all, I do not like to rush. Let me explain the contradiction.

To hike more than thirty miles a day, several unknowns have to come true. The hiker must be in top physical shape and be able to follow one day of strenuous hiking with another. The terrain must allow the hiker to take long strides – the flat Kittatinny Ridge helped me do that, whereas the hand-over-hand climb up Katahdin or sliding through Pinkham Notch on my belly prevents the long strides necessary to make up the distance. The pack must be light – relatively. I would guess my pack weighs less now than at any time, despite my needing to carry three containers of water. Although my pack still weighs more than forty pounds, more than any weekender would want to carry, compared to the loads I carried up north, it's nothing.

After Mark drove me back from his house, I hiked only ten miles, although that included climbing twelve hundred feet out of the Gap. Climbing a mountain no longer concerns me, so I nodded my head and smiled when people coming down the trail warned me about the difficulty of the climb. The climb was steep, in fact, very steep, but it was over quickly. No matter. My concern was more focused on what lay ahead: the questionable availability of water and the unrelenting rockiness of the Trail through Pennsylvania.

Since I first began the hike, I fended off attacks from Northbounders when they learned I come from Pennsylvania, as if I personally cluttered the Pennsylvania Trail with rocks.

"Where are you from?"

"Pennsylvania."

"Your Trail sucks!"

A rocky trail along a ridge or a smooth trail with lots of elevation changes – what difference does that make to a seasoned hiker like me? After all, if it is not one thing, it is another. And even though no stream crosses the top of a ridge, black raspberries do, providing continual refreshment by the handful. And no spring anywhere, not even those sweet ones in Maine, could produce as refreshing a drink as the one I carried with me today.

Although Mark's mother twisted my arm, through the phone, to come to her house for dinner, no matter how many miles I hiked to get there, it was worth it at the end: roast beef, real mashed potatoes – not instant – real cherry cheese cake –not instant – and a real blueberry cobbler for dessert. As they say, "Whatever doesn't kill you makes you fatter."

The best part of the meal was the never-ending supply of fresh mint iced tea. Although Mark's mother brewed tea and crushed mint all night, I could not quench my thirst. She laughed every time I refilled my glass and she made a new batch today for my containers in a futile attempt to satisfy my thirst for her tea on the Trail.

I will move her over to my list of Free Lunches on the AT.

Mark and I stopped at the Omega Health Food Store, where I finally ate one of their renowned whole wheat pizzas, topped with grilled vegetables, avocado, olives, and sprinkled with sesame seeds. The pizza reminded me of all the North-bounders who told me to stop there. The Snail Sisters must have reached Massachusetts by now, perhaps even meeting up with their old friend, Charley Fisher, at the house of the Mystery Woman.

When we first made plans, Mark wanted to take a few days to hike with us, but now he needed to return to Allen-town because of his summer job. That is a shame. I would have enjoyed his company. He is not overly chatty, but makes himself available to share a thought or a view. As an Eagle Scout, he handles himself well in an emergency or when deal-ing with the outdoors.

Apparently, as I have been told, he is not all that tall, but I never noticed because he comes across big. At 5' 4, his favorite sports are swimming, crew, and basketball, sports traditionally reserved for the tallest among us. What he lacks in height, he makes up for in determination and fitness. Crew has a place for short people, in steerage, but Mark rowed, not coxed, for the Virginia crew team. His teammates said, "We're going to call you "Spike," because you were once a tall person who got hammered into the ground." His stature, he could not help, but he excelled at what he could control.

With his other big sport, basketball, he was not as much a player as a super spectator. When tickets for the Atlantic Coast Conference tournament become available each February, students line up on a first-come, first-served basis. For the past two years, Mark was among the first to camp out, several days before the tickets went on sale. He would then participate in the governance of the line, deciding when each person could take breaks to attend classes and blackballing those who did not show up to wait when it was their turn. It takes a different level of fandom to sleep winter nights curled in a sleeping bag on concrete.

When I left Mark at the Gap, I was seventy-three miles northeast of Hawk Mountain, the place of my next rendezvous.

As a kid, I used to go to Hawk Mountain with my father to watch thousands of hawks fly overhead on their annual journey south. On the northern face of the mountain, one could almost touch these birds of prey as they soared overhead on their journey to warmer climates. After two and half months of my own migration, I reached Hawk Mountain where I waited for Geoff Hopkins, my brother-in-law.

I am a Pennsylvanian and I believe a person should be true to their state. I felt strong climbing out of the Delaware Water Gap, but I was unprepared for what lay ahead. Whereas Maine was a never-ending mud bath, after hiking these past few days into Pennsylvania, I wish I were back in Maine. There, I admit it.

The moving ice of the glaciers ground the once massive Blue Mountain in Pennsylvania into a long, flat ridge covered with mountain clutter. After just a few days hiking over these many rocks, I will need to get my shoes resoled again.

On August 9, after climbing out of the Delaware Water Gap, I hiked nine miles to Wolf Rocks – see – they don't even hide the fact there is nothing here but rocks. Yet, despite its name, I found a flat stretch just large enough to unroll my sleeping bag by the side of the Trail, where I cooked dinner, wrote in my journal, read a while, and then enjoyed a pleasant night's sleep. I figured if I could hike twenty-nine miles on the first day and twenty-four on the second, I would cut my last day to just the seven-mile side trail to reach the Hawk Mountain summit by eleven o'clock. This was a huge undertaking, but no worse than my race to the Gap.

I awoke with the sun, but the sky soon became overcast and increasingly threatening. The path was strewn with rocks and with every step, I risked turning an ankle, but I kept going as fast as I could, for as long as I could. I carried a bag of #3 Gorp in my red strap pocket, munching to keep my energy level up. My #3 Gorp, what a weekend hiker would call Trail Mix, combines coconut, raisins, and dates, to go along with mixed nuts. Despite the bad footing, at least the trail ran along the top of the ridge, so I spent none of my Gorp-induced energy on steep climbs.

After covering twenty-two miles by early afternoon, I came down the ridge to a small road that wound downhill toward the village of Wind Gap. With just seven miles left to reach my goal for that night, I thought I would save time by hitching to the village to buy a hoagie, rather than take the time to prepare dinner. I could pick up some additional food to eat on the run as well.

A hoagie is one of those classic Philadelphia foods, served to dock workers, truck drivers, students – and anyone else looking for a big meal, full of flavor, at a low price. The name "Hoagie" derives from the Hog I. (short for island) sandwich. The Hog Island shipyard employed Italian immigrants during World War I, who stuck Italian meats and cheeses, along with a marinated salad – antipasto – on a long Italian roll. Hence, the Hoagie. Jealous New Yorkers, always trying to keep up with their betters to the south, copied the sandwich and called it a "Sub," after its shape. But it just isn't the same.

I hoped Wind Gap, though still two hours north of Philly, fell under the Quaker City's culinary hegemony. I hitched to a shopping strip and entered a pizza parlor with Formica tables and a black and white TV. I could just as well be in Northeast Philadelphia, but of hoagies – they knew nothing. I settled for two pizza slices, then walked to a grocery store to buy some food to last me for my remaining dash to Hawk Mountain. I bought another Philadelphia favorite, Tastykake Krimpets, "made from milk, butter and eggs – all the good things wrapped up in one." I also bought four fresh peaches; unfortunately, I ate these while trying to hitch a ride back to the Trail.

One of the greatest hoagies I ever tasted was made by a man in South Philadelphia, who called himself "Pappa Strano." He was a round guy, with a dark moustache and a bald head, who proudly proclaimed himself the inventor of "The Strano Special," a hoagie made from exotic Italian meats and cheeses, which he heated in a toaster oven and topped with his own secret sauce, before piling on the usual chopped lettuce, tomato, onion, and peppers. It looked great, smelled terrific, and tasted wonderful.

He told us, "I don't care how long the line is; I don't care how many people are standing in front of you; if you want the Strano Special, you walk right up and say, "Make me a

Strano Special." I was with some classmates from Virginia – JT, Ginger, and my doppelgänger, George – on a field trip, studying the various ethnic groups that settled in Philadelphia from the Swedes and Quakers to the panoply of peoples who live there today. Nothing made me feel more proud than to say I was from the same city that hailed an artist like Pappa Strano.

My hike turned ugly on the other side of Wind Gap, when I was attacked by the horde of the flies. When I reached the firebreak, I sat on the top of the ridge with my poncho draped over my head, fly free, but sitting in the rain without a tent. The trees began again on the other side of the clearing, so I dared not re-enter the forest in the rain. I tried to cheer myself by reading Clavell's *King Rat*, proving, once again, that a Japanese prisoner-0f-war camp was a light-hearted romp compared to hiking the Appalachian Trail. There was no sunset under the dark, grey clouds, just a gradual loss of light. I unrolled my sleeping bag on my ground cloth and put my poncho on top of it, missing the tent for the first time since Connecticut.

I thought about tying a tarp between two trees, staking the corners to the ground to form a lean-to. It worked for me in Maine, but if I tried that in Pennsylvania, I would be hard pressed to find enough ground without rocks to stretch out. Perhaps a hammock would come in handy over these rocks, with maybe a waterproof space blanket.

The storm passed during the night and, when I awoke shortly after dawn, the sunrise promised a beautiful day. I crossed the clearing and reentered the woods cautiously. I took one step, then stopped. Waiting, I looked around. I listened for buzzing. Like many devilish things, flies detest beautiful days. Good, because I needed to hike thirty miles just to get myself within striking distance of Hawk Mountain.

I walked quickly all day, but with two gaps to cross, down and then back up, I began to lose steam. I probably felt fatigue due to the stress from my battle with the flies. Although still short of my original goal, I wanted to at least reach the Allentown Lean-to, about a mile past where Route 309 crossed the mountain range, seventy miles north of West Mt. Airy, the Philadelphia neighborhood where I grew up.

I crossed the highway way after dark. Back under the trees, I could not see a thing and worried the grassy jeep road I walked on would again become the treacherous rocky path, making night walking dangerous. I could sleep on the Trail; all I needed to do was unroll my sleeping bag. Yet, falling short of the Allentown Lean-to, would leave too many miles for the next day; I needed to cut the mileage into something manageable. As it is, the lean-to is still five miles short of Dan's Pulpit, my original goal for the night. I was tired from walking all day and it was dark. I gave myself a few more minutes before I would give up trying to find the lean-to in the dark of night. Then, just as I was about to give up, I noticed the faint outline of a path to my left, illuminated by a light. When I turned onto the path, I saw a huge pillar of flame. I followed the flame to the Allentown Shelter. If not for this blaze, I would have missed the turnoff.

As tired as I was, the three yokels who built the bonfire were not ready for bed, nor keen on my falling asleep either. They kept feeding the blaze making the shelter very hot and bright. I could tell from the many bottles of Canadian Club, and the rows of firecrackers, that they were not thru-hikers. Not that firecrackers weigh a lot, but thru-hikers do not carry glass bottles. Every now and then, one of these considerate young men would toss another row of firecrackers into the blaze. I tried to sleep through it all. After all, I have put up with worse things of late.

I awoke shortly after day break, ready to hike the last stretch to Hawk Mountain. Even though I used only my back pad and sleeping bag, I could not believe how much noise I made getting ready to go. Why did those pots keep clanging? Still, it was thoughtful of those nice boys to wake up at dawn to see me off.

I covered the thirteen miles in less than five hours, walking over the rocky path, and climbing the mountain, but I made it, reaching the summit of Hawk Mountain in time to write a few notes in my journal, to reminisce, and to try to get the horror of the flies out of my mind. The scrapes on my legs will heal themselves.

AUGUST 15.

Sweet Home, Philadelphia

I made it to the lookout on Hawk Mountain with plenty of time to meet Geoffrey Hopkins, who then drove me to Pottstown, where he lives with my sister. While my sister and I sat on the couch listening to music, we heard the news that Elvis died. The announcement saddened me, but the mood got even stranger a moment later when the cat sitting next to us, stood up, arched her back, and gave birth to a kitten right there on the couch. If I were superstitious, I would say the kitten contained the immortal soul of Elvis Presley. Fate presented my sister with this once-in-a-millennium chance to name the kitten "Elvis" or "The King," but she named it "Booga Bear"; another cosmic opportunity lost.

The next day, they drove me to Philadelphia. Only the two English Springer Spaniels greeted me when I arrived. There was a third dog when I left for the Trail, a dachshund, but she died during the same July heat wave that forced me out of my shorts in Vermont.

It was murder, actually. A friend of my mother stopped by with a puppy who chased the dachshund around the yard until suddenly, the dog just up and died. My brother, whose dog she was, was off at camp and missed saying goodbye. My father dug a grave for her at the back of our yard, burying her in a dog food bag, because, as he explained, "She always stuck her damned head in the dog food bag."

Despite the comfort of a house with a stove and a refrigerator, I cooked some of the foods I enjoyed on the Trail – with mixed results. This morning, I collected milkweed from Carpenter Woods near our house. I cooked the dish just as I learned from my visit to the Audubon center in Connecticut, sautéing the milkweed in butter, but the season to eat milkweed turns out to be brief. Instead of eating a delicate green vegetable, what I served tasted like the stuffing from a sofa. I retched into the sink and kept everyone else from trying it.

Yesterday, I reproduced the whole-wheat pizza I finally got to enjoy with Mark at the Omega Health Food Store near the Delaware Water Gap. Since it would take a few hours for the dough to rise, I used the time to rebuild the bookshelf in my bedroom. My father built it when we first moved to the house by stacking eight-foot-long planks on bricks as support. I cut the planks in half, stained them and the bricks walnut brown, then set the shelves at right angles in the corner of the room. The new bookcase came out great.

Just before kneading the pizza dough, I noticed my hands were also stained walnut brown. I washed and scrubbed them with soap and water, even using a loofa sponge, but could not make them come clean.

Anyway, the pizza turned out great. I kneaded the whole-wheat dough, chopped fresh vegetables, added chunks of cheese, and sprinkled sesame seeds on top. In the hot oven, the dough baked, the cheese melted, and the vegetables toasted. Everyone loved it.

While we were enjoying the pizza, I glanced at my hands as they approached my face with a slice. They were sparkling clean, but I could not remember how they got that way. Then it struck me: the oil based walnut stain needed an oil based solvent – like a big ball of pizza dough. So, this particular whole wheat pizza came out a tad darker than the one they serve at the Omega Health Food Store.

This will remain our secret.

When I reached Hawk Mountain, I arrived an hour ahead of when I told my brother-in-law to meet me, following three days and one hundred miles of hard walking. There is an element of chance to keeping these appointments. I cannot control trail changes, or the weather, or flies, but I can control what time I set off each morning, how often and for how long I stop, and how intensely I walk. Compared to my first weeks of hiking, I move much faster, hike longer, and take fewer breaks. My strategy for hitting these rendezvous is to hike longer than necessary each of the early days as to cut down the number of miles left to hike on the last day.

I certainly know what it is like to arrive late. For most of my life I have been a late arriver: late for school, late for work, late for dates. I make excuses like the traffic was bad or the bus passed me by. Looking back on a lifetime of excuses, I feel embarrassed. Every time I offered an excuse for my lateness, I reduced myself. I never again want to make excuses. If someone presses me for a reason, I can give one, but there really is only one reason. I made a choice and I lost the bet. If I am late in the future, it is not due to traffic. If I have to get somewhere in the morning and – surprise, surprise – I hit traffic – what am I, stupid? The volume of traffic varies. Timing my trip to arrive just on time, is no different than believing in Santa Claus. Five minutes early is on time; on time is late. I will apologize for disrupting a meeting or for keeping someone waiting, but I will no longer offer an excuse. The reason I am late is I chose not to allow enough time to account for the variability of the journey, or I made the choice to place the task on hand above the appointment I committed to keep.

I carry books with me and I keep this journal. Every time I get somewhere early, I read or write. When I finish this hike, I will continue to take a book with me when I travel. By accepting the existence of variation, I will arrive a few minutes early on most occasions. Since it might rain, or there might be an accident – I will leave time for uncertainties.

On the other hand, I heard that if you don't miss two flights a year, you are spending too much time waiting at airports, so who knows.

AUGUST 16.

Allens Lane

Yesterday, I walked our two English Springer Spaniels around my neighborhood. I will head back to the Trail soon, so I want to implant memories of my upbringing in my brain. These will be the movies I will play to break the monotony of each day's hike. (Someone years from now will ask, "So what did you do on the days off from hiking?" I will answer, "I hiked.")

We wound up at the Allens Lane Art Center, two blocks from my house, where I unleashed the dogs so they could run in the field, the same field where I grew up playing baseball and football.

The first time I played there was when I was six years old, at my one and only day camp experience. At the first game of softball, I ran to third base and announced, "I'm going to play third base, just like my Pop-Pop." When the first batted ball nearly took my head off, the counselors wisely repositioned me to the coveted "back-up right fielder" position, which I played for the remainder of the season.

As the years went by, I learned to play the game. Living just two blocks away, I went there often with my father, who would hit grounders and fly balls to me. This was where the neighborhood kids went for pickup games. Eventually, I got better and by the time I reached high school, I could hit a baseball over the fence into traffic. The screech of a car was reward enough.

When I was fourteen, having just returned from Scout camp, I took the dogs to the field just as I did today. Like today, my hair was longer than usual and my arms and legs showed the effect of weeks of mosquito attacks. I was minding my own business, just like today, watching the dogs chase each other around the field, when four kids on mini-bikes rode up and began circling me.

They got off the bikes and closed in around me. One pulled out a metal comb, called a "pick," and said, "I think I'm going to get me some 'white meat.'" The three other gentlemen laughed at his clever word play. They began pushing and taunting me. I hoped that by not reacting to the taunts, I would avoid escalating the confrontation. But appeasement never seems to work. Emboldened by my passivity, which they took for weakness, one of these young men got down on all fours behind me, so when the leader of the pack pushed, I flipped over the squatter, landing on my back. This enabled these future Rhode Scholars to kick me, while I tried to protect myself on the ground. I did not strike back thinking my non-violence would cause them to lose interest. As it turned out, my withdrawal emboldened them to say or do anything without fear of retribution.

I was not alone while this was happening. Besides my two dogs, who were waiting in the shade near the entrance for me to finish cavorting with my friends, in the other direction, not one hundred feet away, practicing his foul shots, was a kid I went to school with since kindergarten. Whenever I spun in his direction, I could see he was doing his best not to look at what was happening. Maybe all it would have taken was a word to defuse the situation, but he said nothing, too afraid to get involved. He and I would then go through high school after this incident, without him ever again looking me in the eye. As my dad would say, "All it takes for evil to triumph is for good men to do nothing."

I wish human nature is not what it is. I wish we can blame the victim of an attack for the attack itself, that way we never have to get involved. I saw cowardice that day in the unwavering eyes of my former school chum. I cannot even picture the bully, whom I never saw again. But I still remember the disappointment I felt and will always feel in the person whom I once considered a friend.

Most people grow up in homogeneous, that is, racially segregated, neighborhoods. Growing up in West Mt. Airy, one of the few mixed neighborhoods that was not in a rush to shift one way or the other, I never saw Whites physically attack Blacks. The only violence I experienced growing up, and it was not a lot, was either Black-on-White or Black-on-Black. I know that Black-on-Black crime is still a crime; we should never discount crime within a race as if it were not important. Black families want to live in peace too. But the point of stating this difference is to point out that the violence in our neighborhood was instigated by young Black males and, on occasion, young Black females.

Now that I have seen more of the world, I understand that not every neighborhood was like ours. Sure, there were areas where White kids beat up Black kids. Certainly, I have never tried to live an entire life – work, school, or buy a house – as a Black person. I have never felt the loneliness that comes from being the first Black family on a White block or the only

Black kid in what was, until then, an all-White school. But I know what it feels like to be me, a White kid in a racially mixed neighborhood. In my experience, the issue is not about race, but about who felt most secure in their power. Race is used as an excuse; the fundamental instinct in humans is to stand on others to gain power. Separating people into racial groups is about creating allies on the subjugation of one group to another. When Jim Stark moved to Los Angeles in *Rebel without a Cause*, he looked no different than the kids who tormented him. Humans are driven to exert power over each other.

I developed into a pretty "fair country ballplayer," a throw-back phrase I learned from my father. When I reached seventh grade, the teachers allowed us to organize an all-star game against the eighth grade. The teams were supposed to represent the entire grade, but the kids who put themselves in charge did not draft anyone from my homeroom. That was the year the home room sections were based on academic aptitude. It is not always the case that the class with the best students has also the worst athletes; but on average that was the case with us. The two best ballplayers were White -- this cool kid from California, Robert Prescott -- and myself. By excluding our section, the self-appointed organizers practiced racial segregation by fielding an all-Black team.

I did not back down and made the point that my home-room deserved representation in a Seventh versus Eighth grade game. Everyone kept homerun stats that year; mine were among the best (although far short of the very best: Reggie Johnson, Reggie Clark, and Eddie Gibbs.)

Jackie Robinson taught us many lessons; unfortunately, different people took away different meanings. I learned to stand up for the right to be judged by my ability on the playing field and not by the color of my skin. Others learned that as soon as they have the strength of numbers, they can exclude those of a different skin color. It made me wonder whether the social history of our country was not about race or morality, but about who held power.

In the late Sixties, there was an edge of violence at our school. The changing neighborhoods shoved people together, not just from different races, but from different walks of life. Kids were bussed into our school from other parts of the city; not only did they not grow up with the same values as the kids in my neighborhood, their parents were unknown and they, once school let out, were virtually untraceable.

One time I was walking into my homeroom carrying an armload of books. Someone snuck up and pushed me, sending me sprawling forward, my books flying ahead of me into the classroom. I lay on the floor stunned for a moment, then pushed myself up, turned, and chased after the much larger and much older kid, nicknamed "Deadeye"; one of the kids bussed in from another neighborhood. I caught up with him in the hallway and began pummeling him. All three eighth grade classrooms spilled out, jamming the halls. Two of the teachers broke through the crowd to separate us.

Looking back, I realize that incident was not simply about a Black kid suckering a White, but a kid without much sense, finding fun in pushing another kid whose arms were laden with books. It might have been funny if it were part of a *Candid Camera* episode. I recall how I was preoccupied with something or other and was not ready for this humor at my expense. He pushed me, but I responded by pinning him against the wall with blows, a response he did not expect. It was, perhaps, a disproportionate response to his provocation. I landed many punches to his one push, but it was also the last time anyone at that school ever pulled something like that on me. I do not think speaking softly with him would have left the same message. Sometimes you must win the right to negotiate.

Any fight between a Black and a White at my school carried with it greater repercussions than a fight between two Black kids – I never saw a fight between two White kids at the Henry School. The teachers were under a lot of pressure to keep our school stable, which meant making sure incidents did not trigger race riots or a mass exodus, both of which took place in nearby neighborhoods.

The fight ended without further incident. Later, at a school dance, the toughest girl in school, asked me to dance and then told me how much the kids respected me for fighting back. That made me think of my father. He told us stories of having to run to school to avoid the kids attending the nearby Catholic school. I guess that prepared him to fight in two wars but it seems that the need to divide ourselves into groups like this is not a way to create a strong nation.

My ancestors arrived in this country during the 1890s. They fled oppression in Russia, where up until the 1870s, ninety percent of the people were slaves. To divert the attention of the Russian peasants from their miserable condition, the Tsar's secret service fomented hatred against people like my ancestors. The Russian secret service forged a document called "The Protocols of the Elders of Zion." In it, they created a ridiculous story about Jews plotting to take over the world. This same story was used to attack the French reformers of the 1840s.

Instead of focusing on the ruling class who enslaved them,

the Russian people readily engaged in state-inspired attacks against my ancestors who risked their lives to come to this country with no more than a few bags of clothes and some old pictures.

Our family landed at the immigration pier at the end of Washington Avenue in Philadelphia. They quickly shed the past. My family soon came to love everything American. My grandfather, the youngest child in his family and the only one born here, became the ultimate American: he played professional baseball.

He lived the Dream.

But it was not a dream open for all who lived in this country or even those who served in the First World War (or the next one, for that matter.) As a barnstormer, my grandfather played all over the country, providing entertainment in the years before television, or even radio, broadcasts of baseball games. Sometimes, he played against all-Black teams and he shared these memories with his son, my father. The inherent unfairness of segregated baseball struck a chord with my father, who stopped playing baseball in his senior year of high school to pursue his calling fighting for justice for all people in our society. On more than one occasion, my father would quote the Old Testament: "Justice, justice, ye shall pursue."

Living in an integrated neighborhood and sending their kids to public schools, represented a belief for my father and mother, that each person can change the world. As one of the kids who wore the bruises, I did not always understand their passion – but I survived.

AUGUST 17.

West Mt. Airy

Today I walked through West Mt. Airy, toward my elementary school, C. W. Henry. Well, I did not walk to the school, but to the Weavers Way Co-Op, across the street.

Co-Ops define West Mt. Airy. My parents belonged to the first babysitting co-op. Parents would babysit for the children of other co-op members, earning points to take a night out themselves without having to pay for a babysitter. I am not sure why it ended, but it may have something to do with the two occasions when women who sat for us killed themselves – and one killed her own children.

Ralph Waldo Emerson said, "An institution is but the lengthened shadow of one man." Five years ago, a man named Jules Timmerman filled his station wagon with fruits and vegetables to sell in our neighborhood. Nothing unusual about that, plenty of folk hustle to make a buck, but Timmerman was pushing more than fruit. He talked to anyone who would listen about his vision for a community-owned business. A year later, Weavers Way Co-op opened in the basement of the Summit Presbyterian Church, next to where we held our scout meetings. My parents were among the first to join; their membership number is 114. Soon, we filled our cupboards with bags of rolled oats, granola, and sunflower seeds. Every few weeks, one of us would spend a few hours packaging bulk items or slicing cheese as part of our membership responsibilities. Each year, the membership grew and soon the Co-op moved to its own building.

A co-op means more than just another way to buy bulk nuts and seeds. It means that enough neighbors consider their community as something greater than the sum of its houses. The Co-op became the town center. Even though I am now away most of the time, whenever I do shop there, I bump into so many people I know that it takes me an extra hour to shop for groceries.

Not to say all has gone smoothly. Last summer, I stopped in after returning home from college. There were signs advertising a pay-in-advance subscription for Maine Lobsters. If enough people signed up, the Co-op would pay for a shipment of lobsters delivered in time for Father's Day. I paid $24 in cash for six lobsters, enough to feed my family. As much as I love the taste of lobster, I was even more pleased that I could do something like this for my dad.

Last summer, I worked six days a week at Pearson's Sporting Goods store on Chestnut Street. When I finished work, the day before Father's Day, I dashed for home, making the train, and walking the six blocks from Carpenter Lane Station to the Co-op, well before it closed.

I handed my receipt to the cashier, who took it to the floor manager. He took it to one of the guys responsible for the shipment, who came over to see me.

"You're too late. Those lobsters are gone."

"What do you mean, they're gone," I said. "I paid for them in advance."

"You should have been here sooner. I sold them off; I couldn't take the chance they were going to die. That would've been cruel."

This guy's version of compassion reminded me of a button that floated around during the Vietnam War that read, "Support Peace or I'll Kill You."

No other store would resell a food item, already bought

and paid for, on ideological grounds. Nevertheless, I swallowed my anger and frustration, lest I sever my relationship with the Co-op, which would be akin, in my father's words, to "cutting off my nose to spite my face."

I spent the rest of last summer living in the neighborhood, taking the Chestnut Hill Local to my job on Chestnut Street, playing softball at night and on the weekends – basically with Co-op employees and other members – and occasionally going out on dates, mainly with young women I met at the Co-op. So, resigning as a matter of principle would not have served my interests. But that was then and this is now. I went through my mother's shopping list, loaded the bags into my backpack, and hiked the six blocks home.

I walked the same six blocks when I attended elementary school, including when I played the French horn in fourth grade. The case was so large, I needed to bend my arm just to lift it off the ground. The flute would have been a lot smarter at that age. After each block, I set the big black case down to rest my arm. Yep, uphill, through the snow, both ways.

I took up the French horn because that was the instrument my cousin Kenny played at Central High School and in the citywide student orchestra. I loved listening to the low melodious French horn solos when I attended youth concerts at the Academy of Music. On the first day I started playing, I excitedly called my cousin on the phone and said, "Guess what instrument I'm playing." I then played a few notes into the receiver. He guessed, "Is it a trumpet?" The melodious tone continued to escape my lips. After a year of lugging that big case to school, I gave in and switched to the trumpet.

I used to walk home from school with a girl named Maxine Kilson, who was of a different race than I. We went to school together from kindergarten through eighth grade. Growing up where I did, our racial differences never entered our conversations. What did I know of other neighborhoods? Maxine was my social and scholastic equal and, now that I am older, I can now reflect that she would make a good life partner for any man. Her boyfriend at the time was a sweet and courteous fellow also named David, just not me. Martin Luther King dreamed of a day when we would judge each other by the content of our hearts, rather than the color of our skin. I went to school with girls and boys who studied as I did, played as I did, and who succeeded or failed based on their talents and efforts, as I did. But why in West Mt. Airy and so few other places?

My cousin Kenny was a kind, courteous, highly intelligent kid who played a mean French horn. He wore thick glasses and displayed a subtle sense of humor. Instead of a school bus, his daily trip to Central High School was on the Broad Street subway from Center City north to Olney Avenue, passing underneath Philadelphia's most destroyed inner city neighborhoods, destroyed not just because of the deteriorating buildings, but because of the lawlessness and violence that existed on the surface. One day, as he was riding the subway, a fight broke out around him. He was punched in the face, breaking his glasses and lodging glass fragments behind his eye. Not one day in his life did he oppress another person, nor did he ever keep anyone from achieving his or her dreams. He was fatherless by then and his mother worked to keep the family afloat – no one handed them anything.

Why in this great country of ours, should a kid have to fear taking public transportation to school? Why is there a section of a city through which anyone, White or Black, male or female, should fear traveling? Did my cousin get his face punched because his attackers believed striking him would correct some wrong? Or were they raised under such cruel and violent conditions they became immune to empathy? Were they so depraved that punching a stranger – a French horn player, mind you – was as natural as my slapping a mosquito that happened to be at the wrong place – my arm – at the wrong time – when my palm was descending rapidly?

Why was I attacked while standing in the middle of the infield at Allens Lane? I have been trying for years to even that score. I increased my strength, fitness, and hand speed. I trained to fight in a boxing tournament during my first year in college, so I would never again let anyone confuse my preference not to fight with fear. Since I returned home from the Trail, I took the dogs to the same park every morning. "C'mon, Punk. Make my day."

I remember a *Bonanza* episode in which a former tough guy changed his life to live in the image of Jesus. He was working as a hired hand at a ranch, when his old gang rode up to extort money from the rancher and his family. The former gang member stepped out of the ranch house and in a soft voice told his former compadres to depart. The bully, who took over the gang, stepped up and slapped him across the face. "What does your religion say about that?"

"To forgive my brother."

The bully looked back at his three sycophants, shared a laugh with them, then struck again. "And to that?"

"To turn the other cheek."

Really enjoying himself, the tough guy struck a third time. "And to that?"

The former gang member said, "The Lord gave us only two

cheeks," and with that he beat the crap out of the aggressor.

I can question "Why?" all day long. At some point, we must be prepared to fight back.

Growing up in West Mt. Airy, I walked to school, played ball, sat in the orchestra, went through scouts with both Black and White kids. After my hallway altercation as an eighth grader, several teachers asked whether I felt okay. I gave it out more than I received – that day. The adrenalin rush came and went. But I realize now why they were concerned.

I never told my parents about the incident. But if I came home bloodied and bruised, would my parents react by sending me and my two younger siblings to private schools? My dad did not make private school money, so more likely, we would have moved to the suburbs. If my parents moved from Mt. Airy, that would have ended their involvement with the community. As community leaders, if they moved, others would move as well. And if the remaining critical mass of White families moved, then the Black families who sought a relatively peaceful place to raise their children would move as well, as many already sent their children to private schools. I did not understand the dynamics that were taking place in cities across America, but the teachers at our school knew what the loss of the motivated, bright students would have on their careers.

All for the stupid act of one kid.

AUGUST 18.

The Parkway

Although I healed my sores and strains this past week, I made sure to stay active, so when I return to the Trail, I will not lose my conditioning. I need these breaks to let my body parts heal: the blisters on my toes, the strawberries on my back; the chafing between my legs. The sores are my only limitation as leg strength and stamina have not limited me since the early days of Maine. As long as the food and water hold out, I know I can hike all day, regardless of the terrain.

I have never appreciated how much of a walking city Philadelphia is. When you travel to a different city as a tourist, the tendency is to take in as much as possible by foot. In my own city, when I have to go into town, I take the train to the closest stop, do what I came to do, and go home. I am more likely to visit a cathedral in Europe than the one in my own city (although I missed my chance to go to Europe, which explains why I am hiking the Trail). I have wandered around New York and Washington more than I have walked in my native Philadelphia.

I took the train to Center City from the Allen Lane train station, then walked the entire length of The Parkway to the steps of the Philadelphia Museum of Art. I did not run up the steps, like Rocky, whose movie I watched with pride last winter, nor did I lift my hands in triumph and jump around. Rocky ran all the way from South Philadelphia, whereas I walked about a mile from Suburban Station. I gazed down the Parkway toward City Hall, sharing the same view with the "Italian Stallion." From there, Rocky could see the entire skyline of Philadelphia, a remarkable view considering not one building stands taller than the hat on the top of William Penn, the statue atop City Hall.

Today, after looking at the city below me, I turned to face the museum. I went there a few times on school trips, when we wandered the halls, happy for a day off from classes. I would

45

always wander around until I found the huge, colorful Peter Paul Rubens painting called "Prometheus Bound."

A giant golden eagle gripped Prometheus with its two sets of talons, while tearing his liver out with its beak. Prometheus is not standing vertical, like most other depictions of the scene, but is splayed out head first to the viewer, so the image comes right at you, bringing the viewer into the scene. I do not know much about art, but I know when a painting haunts me.

My mom would occasionally dabble with watercolors. She possessed a world of talent, but she never stayed with anything for long. My Dad, to my knowledge, knew nothing about art nor took any interest in it, other than to support the interest of his children.

One day he came home after a day working in the hot inner city and, seeing a paper cup filled with orange juice on the kitchen counter, gulped it down. My sisters screamed for him to stop, but were too late. As they painted, they dipped their brushes into the paper cup. They must have been painting pumpkins or oranges.

Despite not knowing water colors from orange juice, he developed an appreciation for outdoor sculpture, not for the aesthetics, but for how it fit into his world view of social justice.

While killing time before a meeting with the Fairmount

Park Commission, he wandered through the woods near Belmont Hall, coming upon a huge block of granite covered with plaques, statues – and ivy. He wondered why such a significant statue wound up abandoned in the woods. The statue honored "Colored" soldiers who served their country from the Revolution through The Great War.

After some phone calls and fact checking, he learned that the city fathers commissioned this piece in the 1920s to sit on the Parkway, along with the other memorials. But as the memory of the war waned, the city fathers thought the subject matter not fitting for the city's new promenade. So, they offered to stick the monument many blocks south in a neighborhood park called Fitler Square. But the neighbors also objected to the distasteful subject matter. First you let a statue in, then the same kinds of people will want to come see it. And that is how a memorial to those who fought and died to preserve the freedoms of the United States wound up stuck in the woods for fifty years.

My father attended meetings of Black war veterans to raise awareness about the statue and to help them raise money. They succeeded in getting the City to move the statue onto the Parkway. They raised money to restore the piece to its original appearance, as well as to provide a fund for its perpetual care. At one of the meetings, he overheard someone asking, "Who's that light skinned fellow?" None of the Black vets could believe an actual White man, a Caucasian, would take the time to correct an ongoing injustice to Black people – that just doesn't happen. But in my father's view of social justice, each meeting should have been overflowing with both Blacks and Whites.

Above my father's desk in his South Philadelphia office, scrolled on parchment, are the words, "*If I am not for myself,*

*who will be? If I am only for myself, what am I? If not now,
when?"*

    To anyone who exclaims they want to live in a better world,
he would say, "Make it a better world, start today." For Blacks
to be "Free at last," as Martin Luther King dreamed, my dad
encouraged people to not wait for the arrival of another great
person, but to work to improve their own communities now.
The rot and decay of our cities, the overcrowded halls of the
Youth Study Center, the riots on the subways, the killings, the
vandalism, the graffiti are signs, he thought, of hopelessness.
The reaction from the police, the criminal justice system, and
the rest of society, added to the weight of this hopelessness.
My father spent his life trying to break through this stalemate.
    The reform Mayor, Richardson Dilworth, named my father
the first executive director of the first Police Advisory Board
located anywhere in the country. The Police Advisory Board

drew a line between what a police officer can do to keep the peace and what he might do to push us into a police state.

Although my father was a licensed attorney, he worked in a row home in South Philadelphia, not in the tall, air conditioned buildings of Center City, with the fancy restaurants nearby. By day, he walked among the poor and the immigrants on the hot, grimy streets of the inner city, but then would unwind on his drive home along the banks of the Schuylkill River and then under the canopy of the trees that overhung the Wissahickon Drive.

He loved trees, partly because of their color and beauty, as well as their role in the ecology of life, but mostly because of their link to both the past and future. He could stand under the same tree where perhaps stood Benjamin Franklin and he could plant a tree that someday his grandson could bring his children to stand under.

During the Korean War, he and my mother lived in Japan. Later, whenever he travelled, he said he always looked forward to returning to Philadelphia so he could drive through Fairmount Park. Philadelphia has the largest park of any country in the world, much larger than Central Park in New York; in fact, Fairmount Park is larger than the entire country of Monaco, the country that stole our princess, Grace Kelly.

One of the many things my father did in his life was to bring the children who grew up in the inner city to Fairmount Park, so they could walk under the trees, cool their feet in the Wissahickon Creek, play on its banks, and gain a respect for nature. You may say he wanted the next generation of voters to value the same natural resources he loved, but he also wanted nature to work its healing on this generation, who needed healing so much.

AUGUST 19.

The Aqueduct

I took a walk through the Wissahickon Woods today, the part of Fairmount Park closest to my house in Philadelphia. I am always impressed by the natural beauty of the park, located within the third largest city in America. W. C. Fields left word that his tombstone should read, "All things considered, I'd rather be in Philadelphia."

That is so funny I forgot to laugh.

W. C. Fields was not the only famous person to go through here. Maybe an outsider would think William Penn is the most famous Pennsylvanian, but he is mostly invisible. Growing up in Philadelphia, we go to the Franklin Institute, run along the Ben Franklin Parkway, quote sayings from Poor Richard's Almanac, but our only observation of Penn is from far below his statue atop the tower of City Hall. Our major university is the University of Pennsylvania, but even that has nothing to do with Penn; it was founded by Franklin. For that matter, the name Pennsylvania was not even for William Penn, the founder, but for his father, Admiral Penn. William Penn changed his religion and became a Quaker, causing him to fall out with the Church of England. Perhaps his only influence at the University of Pennsylvania is the name of the sports teams, The Penn Quakers.

So, on the surface, at least, we are much more Benjamin Franklin's town, than William Penn's, although the latter influences us in the laws and customs that gird our society.

William Penn was arrested in England because of the laws prohibiting people to gather unless in the presence of a minister of the state religion, which the Quaker Penn was not.

After he was acquitted by a jury, the Mayor of London ordered the jury imprisoned until they changed their verdict. Penn encouraged them to resist. Today, in America, we have the right to assemble, we are free from the abuse of a state religion, and we have an impartial jury, free from government control.

We were different from other countries: we can assemble peacefully; we can worship as we wish; we can criticize our government, its laws and treaties, and even our elected and appointed leaders; and we can even make fun of their big ears, their ski slope noses, or their sexual proclivities.

This country belongs to each one of us, passed down from one generation to the next. It is not enough to protect this dream from foreign threats, we must defend it against people who go into government service to satisfy their own needs over the needs of the citizenry. It is also our responsibility to speak out against those who pervert their position, not just for personal financial gain, but for the pleasure of exercising power over the lives of others. It is our responsibility to make sure the police we hire to protect and serve us do not abuse their positions. The challenge to protect our liberty falls not just on the government, but on us all. For, as my father used to say, "The price of liberty is eternal vigilance."

What most visitors do not see when they pass thorough Philadelphia on their way to somewhere else, is the beauty of Fairmount Park with its rushing streams, steep ravines, waterfalls, and stone bridges. I grew up near the park and spent a great part of my life on its trails and paths.

I often entered the woods under the McCallum Street Bridge, a high arched steel bridge that spans the Cresheim Creek. My two springer spaniels, Misty and Abigail, would dash down the steep slope under the bridge to reach the creek;

perhaps this is how I learned to leap down steep slopes.

Although there are many different paths to choose among, I usually run a route that would take me about five miles up and down slopes and along ridges. When I run, Abigail, whom I affectionately call Ralph, will run along with me, while her mother, Misty, will hang around the first stone bridge and wait for us to come back, greeting us with a gentle scolding for having left her alone for so long.

The path winds along the Creishem Creek until it reaches a stone bridge, where it crosses and continues along until Devil's Pool, a deep cove in the rocks where generations of kids have plunged into the deep, clear water. From there, the trail turns south along the creek on its way to meet the Schuylkill River. The trail also heads north from Devil's Pool, across a high wooden bridge and along a ledge of rock and dirt overlooking the valley.

Sometimes, I might not cross the first bridge, but instead turn right, climbing up a steep ridge overlooking the historic Valley Green Inn, where George Washington may have slept – or maybe not.

The Cresheim Creek, as well as the many other creeks in Fairmount Park, is lined with stone walls, the remains of the dozens of mills built over the first two hundred years of the colony's existence, when water power served as the main source of energy. These mills provided the industry that turned Philadelphia into the world's second leading commercial center.

As the city grew, so did its water needs. The City built the Water Works on the banks of the Schuylkill River to pump water to a reservoir, where now sits the Philadelphia Museum of Art on the Parkway. To secure the purity of the water, especially after several outbreaks of diseases, the city preserved thousands of acres of land upriver to form Fairmount Park. This preservation ended the mills and that way of life, but other energy sources were already transforming industry.

Last summer, I stayed home, while the rest of my family drove to Florida; I took the dogs to the woods on a nightly basis to run up and down the trails.

One hot and muggy July night, we ran to the left of Devil's Pool in the direction of the Schuylkill River instead of our usual loop north to the Valley Green Inn. We ran along a narrow path, just below the top of the ridge, sometimes with me in the lead and sometimes Ralph leading me.

Misty, her mother, stayed behind. Although she was never much of an athlete, she produced two litters of eleven pups in all. There was a twelfth, but it came out stillborn. My mother took it out of the litter box and we buried it in the backyard. When we returned, Misty went upstairs to my sister's room to bring a doll to her litter box, a hard substitute for her deceased puppy.

Ralph was her first-born and the one we kept. Ralph legally belonged to me. I paid for the breeding, using my entire fortune built through weekly deposits of spare nickels and dimes, most of which I earned finding and returning soda bottles to Pera's, the local grocery a few blocks from our house.

When the City began drawing water from the river, it discovered that as people moved in along the watershed, they spewed waste into the creeks and streams. Banning development in the park was one step, the other was to construct a wastewater pipeline that went along the ridge, sometimes submerged under the dirt path, other times serving as bridges over ravines. These concrete aqueducts, built a century ago, are wide enough to run across, but tell that to Ralph.

We came upon a particularly long stretch of exposed concrete, bridging a steep ravine. I ran across, but Ralph hit the skids and stopped at its edge. I went back, encouraging her to come, but she would not step foot on the barrel-shaped, concrete bridge.

I grabbed her collar and dragged her a few feet, but when I let go she turned around and ran back to the dirt path. I ran back and forth showing her it was wide enough for her to run on without falling off. She would not budge.

I went back and picked her up, carrying her to the halfway point.

"We are halfway," I said. "Now finish this on your own." I put her down but she spun around and ran by me all the way to the path.

"What is this, *A Night at the Opera*?"

I ran back to her. This time I put my hands on either side of her and lifted her front paws off the ground. Straddling her, I waddled down the aqueduct so she could see she would not fall off. At first, she resisted, but after crossing halfway, she began moving her legs. I let her go and she continued to run forward until she got to within ten feet of the end. Then she jumped off.

I ran to the end and called to her; she did not come. I did not hear a thing. Meanwhile, it was getting dark.

"Good Grief," I said, as I climbed down the steep slope. I was concerned she hurt herself jumping from the aqueduct, which was about six feet above the ground at that point. But when I got to the area where she must have landed, there was no sign of her. I called for her and looked in the brush and bramble. I was getting scratched by the wild roses and was sure I was walking though poison ivy. My only cover was my running shorts, socks and running shoes.

I brushed against stinging nettle which caused the skin on my side to become red and swollen. The burning sensation shot up my body, causing my cheek to twitch.

I could not believe how quickly she vanished. Her anxiety over crossing the aqueduct must have sent her running back to where we left Misty. We were several miles away, so I climbed back on top of the aqueduct and ran back in the direction I came. I ran along the ridge until I came to Cresheim Creek, and then ran along the creek, calling for her as I ran. No one else was on the path as the sun sunk behind the ridge. By the time I reached the spot where we left Misty, it was pitch black in the woods. Misty was there barking, pacing back and forth, looking very cross at me. I looked expectantly for Ralph, but she was not there. I gathered the leashes and walked home.

I went to bed early, setting my alarm. I would get up at daybreak and search for her the whole day.

My room was on the third floor of the house. We did not have central air conditioning, but my parents finally relented and installed a window unit in my room. I swore that when I have a son of my own, I would never force him to sleep at the top of an old house without an air conditioner.

During the night, the heat and humidity broke, and it rained with fury. I slept fitfully, waking often to look at the clock, waiting for daylight. I felt terrible, not just for Ralph's sake, but for mine. If you own a dog, and really open that door to your life, you realize that the care you get from a dog is always greater than the care you give to her.

When I sat at my desk, she would curl up against my feet, keeping them warm during the winter. She was also my protector. There were times during high school when I stayed out Sunday afternoons, and when I returned home, Ralph would sniff a strange scent – her competitor. When I first brought her rival Stacy to visit our home, Ralph lunged for her, teeth bared, with one desperate attempt to chase away this wicked woman, this temptress. She spent the rest of the evening under a living room chair, seemingly muttering to herself. Eventually, she reasoned that since I always did come home, perhaps this Stacy was no real match. Good ol' Ralph.

Through the long night, I tossed and turned, wracked by dreams of falling, of drowning, and of wildly searching. Then, still sound asleep, I turned in bed and my hand slipped off the side. I imagined my hand fell onto something wet and furry. I dreamed I was holding and petting Ralph. I dreamed she licked my arm and then my face. I opened my eyes and there she was. I awoke. How did she find her way back home? How did she get into a locked house? She climbed onto the bed, soaking wet and covered with dirt, but I held onto her as we both slept off a long and troubling night.

I learned a few days later that she sat howling outside our door to get in, while the air conditioner over my bed drowned her out. Sleeping with their window open, our neighbors heard her loud and clear; Mr. Saurbrey, who possessed a spare key, let her into our house so he and his wife could go back to sleep. Where Ralph ran to after leaping from the aqueduct, or how she found her way home, I will never know.

AUGUST 20.

The Pinnacle

I started today's hike in the town of Eckville, down the road from Hawk Mountain. Now, I am writing in the evening on a cool day, with not even the hint of a cloud in the sky. On such a day, only the horizon blocks my view. I began this third part of my journey accompanied by my father who drove me back to the Trail from Philadelphia. He hiked two miles with me before turning back. His face was full of excitement as he walked by my side. I could tell he was walking the rest of the way to Georgia with me, in his mind.

A day like this could lure anyone into hiking. The sky is dark blue and the first few miles along the graded dirt trail made the hike an effortless stroll.

This was not the first time I hiked out of Eckville. Last summer, my buddy Mark hiked with me on the stretch of Trail from the Allentown Lean-to to Port Clinton. Although Mark was a sturdy and experienced hiker, his shoes were not. He suffered miserably over the last fifteen miles. Putting on the pair of boots that stripped his feet raw, took a lot of courage, as I would later know firsthand.

I bought my heavy hiking boots a few months ago, thinking a lighter boot would fall apart over the rough terrain of the Trail and would not provide my ankles with the lateral support they would need, especially given the extra weight I would carry with the big pack. Conventional wisdom suggests a light boot would give way when twisted, whereas a heavy boot would not. Perhaps after five months of hiking the lighter shoe would have fallen apart, but with my heavy boot, my feet fell apart. By the end of most days I felt like I was lifting concrete blocks with every step. Maybe a lighter, less expensive pair would have worn out. If so, I could have thrown them away in favor of a new pair. Now, it costs me to put new soles on because the boots cost too much to discard. Moreover, keeping my ankles stiff means my knees absorb more of the shock from each step, which is why I periodically must wrap my knee in an Ace bandage (whenever I am not using it to repair my pack frame.)

When Mark and I finally reached the Port Clinton Hotel, we went inside to wait for Mark's father to drive us back to Allentown. Almost every small Pennsylvania town has its hotel, but the one in Port Clinton is a favorite among Thru-hikers because of its homemade soup. When we reached Port Clinton, Mark wanted a chair, whereas I headed for the toilet. Mark took a seat at the bar and ordered a soda.

"Don't you want a beer?" I could hear the hefty proprietress ask from where I sat.

I knew Mark would prefer a beer, but he grew up in Pennsylvania where the legal drinking age is twenty-one. Although he bought beer legally in Virginia, as an Honor man, he could not lie about his age just to get a drink in Pennsylvania.

"Well, yes, but no."

"What do you mean," questioned the man across the horseshoe-shaped bar. "Do you want one, or don't you?"

"Well, sure I want one, but I'm not old enough to drink – legally."

"You old enough to fight for your country?" the bartender asked.

"Why, yes, I suppose."

"Then you're old enough to drink," she said, pouring Mark a beer.

When I emerged, I skipped the preliminaries and went straight to the finals.

I experienced another underage drinking scene over Spring Break last year after getting together with the girl I took to my high school prom. She attends Penn State while I, of course, attend The University of Virginia, but our spring breaks coincided last year. I was a month shy of my twentieth birthday and she was almost nineteen, having skipped a year of school. The waitress asked us, "Would you care for a drink?"

Now, as I mentioned, the drinking age in Pennsylvania is twenty-one. We were both in college, so we were no strangers to someone handing us a drink, but the chance to get served at a real restaurant, in downtown Philadelphia, took us by surprise. Our eyes met. Erica – ravishingly beautiful, elegant, stylish, and sophisticated – said, with a wave of her hand, "I'll have a sangria."

Neither stylish nor sophisticated, I looked down the list of beers. But then Erica thought, "Hey, if I'm going to get served, I might as well go all the way."

"On second thought," she told the waitress, "I'll take a die-queery."

The waitress stared at her for a moment and then said, "You mean a daiquiri?"

Needless to say, it was ginger ale for us that night.

Memories like these fill the hours when one hikes alone. I remembered Mark and I ate lunch at The Pinnacle, an outcropping of rocks with caves to explore and chimney-like rock formations to climb. As I neared The Pinnacle this time, I passed a number of disgruntled hikers walking toward Eckville.

"If you're planning to camp at The Pinnacle, you might as well turn around now. There's some fatso, Elmer Fudd, kicking everyone out of the area."

Up ahead a jeep followed another group of hikers. I kept walking.

The Jeep, with "Watershed of Hamburg" written on the door, stopped next to me and the hefty warden lowered his window.

"Where do you intend to camp tonight, son?" he asked.

"Pocahontas Spring."

He raised his eyebrows and said, "Pocahontas Spring is seven miles from here and it's already past four."

"Don't worry. I'm a Thru-hiker; I'll make it."

A Thru-hiker has a look about him: Desperation? Fatigue? Insanity?

The view from The Pinnacles was outstanding. What a great place it would have been to spend the night. But I moved on, not wanting to explain to Elmer Fudd why I did not make Pocahontas Spring. I walked a mile farther to Pulpit Rock, before stopping again to enjoy another great view. Although the entire stretch from The Pinnacle to Pulpit Rock was typically Pennsylvania rocky, in another 100 yards I reached a grassy knoll, a perfect place to stretch out for the night. Unfortunately, there was an observatory on the knoll – and a road leading to it. I stashed my pack in the woods and then walked back to Pulpit Rock to cook dinner and read until it became too dark for the wide warden of Hamburg to chase me away. Later, I unrolled my sleeping bag behind the observatory on the grassy knoll and fell asleep watching the stars.

I have been giving thought about the forces that have shaped my life. I have directed my life as much as a leaf driven by the wind determines its own direction. For that matter, I let someone else determine how I would spend half a year; which is why I slept alone on a grassy knoll behind an observatory in rural Pennsylvania.

The Trail was supposed to be the chance to step off the merry-go-round, call a time out, to watch from the outside for a while. Over the months on the Trail, I looked at my life as I look at the stars above – as a distant observer – trying to figure everything out from a distance. Timeouts are essential in any game, but they should be followed with engagement – and soon thereafter. I am already feeling anxious, this sitting on the sidelines. I have never been one to sit on the bench, waiting to jump back in.

When we reached our first lean-to in Maine we were greeted by two guys who met in Viet Nam. I guess part of me viewed hiking the Trail as a form of penance for not going to Viet Nam. Marring my eighteenth birthday was the sickening image of the last Americans scrambling aboard the last helicopter leaving Saigon from the roof of the embassy. The Trail is teaching me how to live with deprivations and physical hardships – without the Punji traps.

I am just a bit too young to have benefited from that

wonderful opportunity to serve my fellow man. In fact, I am one of the relatively few people in my generation not to register with the Selective Service. Congress gave us ninety days before our eighteenth birthdays to register. I felt no compulsion to be the first to register, so I figured I would wait to the ninetieth day. During those three months, Congress ended Selective Service.

My thoughts are never about hiking when I walk. Long distance hiking is a great challenge, a grinding test of endurance, but at some point, it becomes a waste of time – at least for me. I no longer see it as a means of finding myself, but a delay in accomplishing what I want to do. I have sustained all the introspection I can take – I itch to get back to my life. I want to complete the Trail, or rather, to be able to say "I completed the Trail," but I have no desire to spend any more of my life walking it.

I did not feel that way when I was home last week, but that may have been because I spent the time productively: painting shelves, reading an excellent book on writing, *Elements of Style*, and considering a speed reading course for when I am done. I ate well, filling myself with the meat and vegetables I have missed on the Trail, while at the same time shunning the white food groups of rice, potatoes, and pasta, which have filled me with hollow calories on this journey. I did pushups and pull ups on the Par Course along the Wissahickon Creek to rebuild my upper body strength.

And then I returned to the Trail.

There is home, which I love, and there is school, which I love even more. In any normal year, I would still be home now, but getting ready to return to school. Living at school and taking classes are two different things. In class, I have weaknesses which I must correct – I realize now the professors will not do this for me. I have to learn to write better. I must be able to read all the assigned readings, in time, and remember what I have read. I did not have these skills coming into college, but I will no longer blame my high school; instead, I will take responsibility for correcting my deficits.

I suffer from my own form of mental slavery, because I waited for others to fix the things that were wrong with me. I will never again wait for someone else to heal me. I will either fix it or move on; no more wailing about how others have let me down.

There are many people to whom the Wizard of Higher Education has granted a piece of paper with the word "Diploma" on it. And there are educated people without those pieces of paper. During these next two months, instead of walking to Georgia to prove some obscure point, I could use the time to learn to write better, increase my reading speed, maybe pick up the trumpet again, rebalance my body, and acquire knowledge in subjects useful for my life.

If I quit the Trail now, I still have time to get back to school, although I would need a place to live, since I sublet my room for the semester. I sacrificed a semester at UVA to hike the Appalachian Trail alone. What did I do to deserve this punishment?

I wanted to spend a semester in England, but after two years of school, I am not sure I would want to miss a semester in Charlottesville. But back a year ago, without a minute's thought, I agreed to forfeit a semester at my heaven on earth to hike the AT, signing away the rights to my room to someone who will spend the following semester in England. Was there no chance I might choose to hike just through August? What a *stunad* I am. Now here I am on a forced exile, my linear Elba, alone, not growing, not engaging with my world.

Yep. I made a really bad choice.

CHAPTER TWO

Helpful

AUGUST 21.

Route 183

I met two guys this afternoon who were out walking for the day. Since the Trail ran over a Pennsylvania state game land jeep road, the three of us could walk side-by-side. Al Brennan and John Bambrick, who must be in their thirties, invited me to join them for dinner, picking up the tab. They entertained me with far more stories than I told them. We went to the Summit View Inn on Rte. 183, one of those gems the locals know about and outsiders blur past. The salad bar included a surprisingly large number of choices, including warm homemade bread. John and I ate the special – turkey with stuffing for $3.75. Of course, we drank a few beers, too.

I sound like my father by naming every low-price I ever paid for a meal. We used to go to the Warwick Hotel in Phila-delphia once a year for my grandmother's birthday. It was the six of us in my family, my grandmother, plus my uncle's family, making twelve in all. The Sunday dinner buffet at the Warwick consisted of three long tables. The first held every appetizer imaginable, including bowls of peeled shrimp (peeled, mind you), platters of clams and oysters on the half shell, smoked oysters, antipasto, chowder, and lobster bisque. After five or six plates of that, I would then turn to the main table, which held carving stations of roast beef and turkey, pots of lobster Newburgh, a giant tray of wonderful chicken potpie – my favorite – although my dad did not want me to fill up on something we kept in the freezer. Then, the third table, filled high with desserts, such as the fixings for ice cream sundaes, and little pastries glazed to look like yellow baby chicks and green frogs. We would find hardened versions of these in my little sister's dresser months later.

My Nana would order a drink called a Pink Lady, something to this day I never heard another person order. They certainly didn't serve these at frat parties.

We stopped going to this legendary feast after they raised the prices to six dollars for adults and three for children. My father explained that when he was a kid, his dad could take his whole family – he and his brother Edward, his mom and dad – to Fisher's Restaurant, where his father paid six dollars for all of them, and that included a lobster for his mother, my Nana. That taught me the principle that after forty years, one cannot spend more on one person's dinner than what one's dad paid for the entire family. By extrapolation, I must stop going out to eat when the bill reaches twenty-four bucks an entree. (Although in my father's defense, they charged my older sister the adult rate.)

I shared with John and Al my story of getting served beer at the Port Clinton Hotel with Mark last year. I am twenty years old and still not old enough to drink in most states along the Trail, yet not once has anyone asked me to see my ID. I would have stopped by the Port Clinton Hotel today, but was not ready to drink a beer at 8 AM, just to prove I could get served there a second time.

When I returned to Mark's house in Allentown last year, we saw the news on TV of the mysterious epidemic that struck the American Legion Convention held at the Bellevue Stratford Hotel in downtown Philadelphia. Several of the attendees died. Mark's mother did not want me to return home, in case the disease was spreading throughout the city, but I said I could not abandon my family, so I went back regardless of the danger. I saw myself as the character in *The Plague* by Camus; I needed to go back to help my family escape. It turned out there was something wrong with the old hotel's air conditioning system, so there was no outbreak of the plague, which left me oddly deflated.

After dinner, John and Al drove me back to the Trail. So here I am, writing under the light of my candle lantern, as the rain begins to fall. I have rebuilt my portable lean-to, using my ground cloth and my poncho. I can avoid the worst of the rain, so long as I do not extend my legs. As great as I felt hanging with those two, I feel even lonelier now, crouched as I am in the woods.

If not for the thru-hiker warning signs – the huge blue pack, the ten weeks since shaving, the massively muscled legs – strangers would not ask me to dinner. So, I have that going for me. But, then again, if I were not doing this, I would be doing something else.

If I could possess one super power, the one I would choose (besides creating world peace, of course, that goes without saying, although I am a realist) would be the power to live in a parallel universe, so I could follow two courses of action at the same time, then select the one that worked best. Sort of like playing "Best Ball" with life. That would be great. I could see how my life turned out by spending five months hiking the Trail and the same five months if I never said yes to Rand's offer. Did I mention this was never my dream?

An old Chinese story explains how difficult it is to know the consequences of our actions. As I recall: A farmer's horse drops dead, the villagers give him another horse; his son falls from the horse and breaks his leg. Each time one of these events occur, the farmer refuses to judge whether it was bad or good, knowing life has to play itself out. When his son broke his leg, the townspeople said "That's bad." The farmer said, "We'll see." A day later, the army came through town conscripting the young men. They did not take the son because of this leg." "That's good," the townspeople said. "We'll see," said the farmer.

Perhaps some good will come from my hiking the Trail, rather than spending the semester traveling through Europe. Perhaps the same amount of good would have happened if I went to Europe for a semester. "We'll see," I guess.

Unlike tonight's cramped attempt to avoid the rain, I spent last night stretched out on the grassy knoll by the observatory, falling asleep under a canopy of stars, that is, until the sound of car doors woke me. A bright light hit my eyes, but then went out. It did this several more times, but no one noticed me. Then I heard a low rumble. The observatory dome opened and a light pierced the darkness. As the light grew, I could see the outline of the telescope. The star gazers stopped talking and the woods became silent again; then, the light went out.

The air was clear and the sky full of stars. And I went back to sleep unobserved.

After I left the grassy knoll this morning, I spent the day alone until I met John and Al. I passed a few people heading north, but no one resembling a Northbounder. Tomorrow, I will eat dinner with people again, if I can find my way to Camp Eagle Springs.

AUGUST 24.

The Counselor Gets Counseled

The alarm rang at 7:15; time to start a new day. Edward French – "Frenchy" – hopped across the cold cabin floor, the first to reach the bathroom. While the other campers dressed, a line formed by the bathroom door. I sat on the edge of my cot rubbing my eyes – How did I just become a camp counselor?

The social agency my father runs in South Philadelphia operates a camp for kids. He and Don Hamilton, the director of Lighthouse Settlement, which runs Camp Eagle Springs, became friends over many years of meetings. Although I never met them, Mr. and Mrs. Hamilton live in Germantown, near the Maplewood Mall, a side street where young entrepreneurs have opened cafés in what was an abandoned retail district.

I awoke on the 22nd of August at daybreak, thinking I would hike twenty-four miles to the Rausch Gap Lean-to, "The Hilton on the AT," as we Thru-hikers call it. It stormed all night and I spent the morning walking in a thick fog. This was the first time I slept in rain since Wind Gap. Although I do not need the extra weight of a tent, the limitation of my poncho and ground cloth left me with the Hobson's choice of sleeping and staying dry with my legs curled or stretching my legs but soaking my sleeping bag. I reached a poor compromise; I did a little of both and began my walk both wet and cramped.

I reached Swatara Gap after eighteen miles of hiking in rain and over the rock infested trails, grinding my third set of Vibram soles. It was yet early on an otherwise miserable day, so I found a pay phone in the back of a store, just off where a highway crosses the Trail. Not knowing the camp's phone number, nor even its locality, made calling a challenge. I leafed through the phone book, looking for either Eagle Springs Camp or Camp Eagle Springs. Pulling a blank I tried the operator, who asked for a locality. Pine Grove stuck in my mind and I lucked out.

I called the camp and asked for Don Hamilton. When he got on the line, he seemed anxious to see me, although a little surprised I called from Swatara Gap, since the closest point to the Trail was back at route 183, where I ate dinner the night before. Although this was not intentional on my part, after all, a Thru-hiker never misses the chance for a free dinner, I mistakenly thought the camp was west, not east, of the highway from where I called. Since I did not want to miss staying at the Rausch Gap Lean-to – "The Hilton on the AT" – I thought I would get within striking distance, dash off for a free dinner, then get back to the Trail in time to hike the last few miles to the famous lean-to.

Despite the added distance, Don graciously sent one of his assistant directors to bring me to the camp twenty miles out of the way, just to give me a free dinner. That also would mean someone would have to drive me back so I can spend the night at the famous lean-to, although it would have to be early, as I did not want to hike over the rocky Pennsylvania trail in the dark.

While I was eating dinner, an assistant director, Annette Fluhr, someone from my neighborhood, sat down beside me and asked, "How would you like to work here?"

"I thought the meal was free. My dad's a friend of Don Hamilton and he said I could stop by for dinner."

"Don't worry, we're not making you work for your dinner. It's just we're short a few counselors and hoped you could help us out for a few days."

It turned out they were in a bind. One counselor left for a few days to take his dental school entrance exams. That they expected. What caught them unprepared was his co-counselor suffered an eye infection, forcing him to leave camp too.

"Hey, I'd really like to help out, really I would, but I'm a Thru-hiker. If I don't reach Virginia by the beginning of September, I won't make it to Springer Mountain before the snow."

"Well, we can't force you. Enjoy your stay."

This left a bunk of nine men ranging from twenty-three to forty-six years of age without a counselor. Concerned over the camp's predicaments and not wanting to alienate anyone from giving me a ride back to the Trail, I agreed to spend the night in the bunk. At least that would give them another day to figure things out. I felt bad turning them down, but I have a Grail to follow. And if they get me back after dinner the next day, I could still spend the night at The Hilton on the AT.

I recognized a lot of people from my neighborhood, West Mt. Airy. Several talented musicians, like Chet Brown, Joel Levine, and Hankus Netsky, work at the camp. Chet Brown is the most polished singer from our neighborhood. Hankus Netsky introduced me and hundreds of other students at my high school to the big band sound of yesteryear as the student director of the Central High Jazz Band. And Joel Levine, besides having the biggest feet of any human being, can play two recorders at the same time, which means he also has one of the largest mouths too.

Several other staff, like Maddy Fluhr and Martha Claffin, sat near me in the Henry School orchestra, where I once played the trumpet. (When I write that the most talented musicians from my neighborhood work at this camp, I am not including myself in that description.)

Eagle Springs is a camp for adults with developmental disabilities. The campers come from all over: some from institutions like Pennhurst, some from group homes, others from their parents' homes. They need a recommendation to attend, guaranteeing they can function in a camp setting. Of the men in my bunk, all have jobs and live either independently or in group homes. They may not be the most intellectual bunch of guys in the world, but they were all friendly and excited I agreed to join them for the night.

After dinner, I walked around the camp while everybody else attended the social. Why would I want to see a bunch of people with disabilities dance? But since I have tired of walking alone in the woods, like the monster in *Young Frankenstein*, I was drawn to the music. I wandered over to the open-air pavilion to watch from outside. Inside danced people, many of whom lived their lives in institutions. My sister, who works in this field, told me that life in an institution, no matter how well intentioned, was so devoid of stimuli that if you placed a normal child in one, he would lose his ability to function normally within a year. I watched from outside as these people – so strange to me – enjoyed themselves. At the start of each song, they would cheer, as if this song was their favorite.

The floor was packed with dancers. Even the campers standing along the walls, perhaps physically not able to dance, laughed and sang with each new song, while tapping their feet to the music. Instead of depression and self-pity, the room was filled with the enjoyment of life.

I watched as a young man tried to ask the much older lady standing next to him to dance. When he would turn to her, she would turn to him, but he would lose his nerve and turn back. I could see the whole thing playing out before me. I wanted to give him some encouragement, shout a few pointers, but I was on the outside. Finally, he asked her. She threw her arms around him, kissing him on his cheek; then the two whirled off. I decided it was time to come inside.

I felt out of place at first. I looked around for someone to dance with and saw a girl counselor I did not know, dancing with several campers. I waited until the song ended, then asked her to dance. We jitterbugged to a Boz Scaggs number.

"Wow!" she said. "You're good. What bunk are you in?"

"What?"

"Who's your counselor?"

"My counselor? Oh, for goodness sake."

The next morning I was the counselor, agreeing to stay until the end of the week, when the soon-to-be dentist returned. While I sat with my bunk at breakfast, several of the other counselors came over to congratulate me on the promotion from camper.

The IQs of these campers fall within the somewhat less than normal range. Still, I was amazed at how capable they are. One of my campers, Eddie Styers, told me, "I have a real important job. I work for Macke."

"What's Macke?"

"That's where they eat at Temple University. Me and George got important jobs there."

"What do you do that's so important?"

"I scrape food off dishes and put them on the rack."

"You torture dishes? I mean, you do this three times a day, every day of the week?"

"Uh-uh, I don't work Sundays."

"You know something, Eddie, you are important. No college graduate could do the job you're doing."

His friend George Johnson also works at Macke; his job is to load racks of dirty dishes into the dishwasher. This was George's second year at camp. He assured me "If you need to go someplace, just ask me. I know this place like the back of my hand."

Aside from his inability to remember anything, George could easily pass in the real world. He looked and sounded like Jethro from the Beverly Hillbillies.

Eagle Springs gives its campers ten days of games, sports, and social activities. For many, this is the only place where people treat them with respect, even deference. Unfortunately, camp does not last long enough to change the neglect of a lifetime.

At every meal, the nurse hands each counselor a packet containing the campers' prescribed medication. Even though I feel the purpose of most psychotropic medication is to help society avoid dealing with people – don't forget, I am an expert on these matters, having read *One Flew Over the Cuckoo's Nest* in Maine – I abided by the camp's policy. Besides, ten days of reality would not greatly alter their lives. But no sooner did I resign myself to comply, then I noticed that George, the closest thing to an athlete in our bunk, needed the support of two friends to get out of his chair.

"What's up, George?"

"I don't know. My foot must have fallen asleep."

I wasted no time getting the nurse's attention. She said George was on four Thorazines a day. I checked the huge pharmacy book she kept on her table. Thorazine is a powerful sedative used to suppress seizures and aggressive behavior. "George," she said, "has no history of either."

I got to the bottom of the mystery from Eddie Styers. George shares a rooming house with Eddie and a few other friends. They each give their paychecks to the landlady, who gives them a weekly allowance. According to Eddie, the landlady increased George's medication because he was "bad." Apparently, George cashed his last check himself to buy going away gifts for his friends. The landlady, in an effort to correct such wayward behavior, took him to a new physician, who raised George's dosage of Thorazine.

Barbara Wagner, my unit leader, got hold of George's regular doctor, who went apoplectic that another doctor would quadruple George's dosage. This is going to get ugly.

Once free of the drugs, George renewed his womanizing.

"See that girl over there? Cute, huh? That's my girl; we're going to get married."

"That's great. What's her name?"

"Hmm . . . I don't remember."

By the second day as counselor, the only two people in my bunk who did not have girlfriends were myself and Sam, my newly-assigned assistant, who dwells in the shady world between counselor and camper. I liked the girl counselors at camp; they were cute and friendly, and some I have known from back home, although it has been years since I saw any of them. Man, I longed to hold one in my arms, but I never did. Some counselors need lessons from campers on how to express their desires.

A few of us counselors teased Frenchy over his latest romance – this one only two days after his old flame left for home. Frenchy grew heated from the kidding and turned to us.

"What's the matter with you guys? A fellow needs to have someone to talk with; can't a fellow have someone to keep him from being lonely?"

I shut my mouth fast. You know, Frenchy, you are right. If only I were as eloquent.

AUGUST 25.

The Hilton on the AT

Back when I was sitting by Finnerty Pond in Massachusetts, reading *The Course of Modern Jewish History* by Howard Sachar, and finishing off the rest of my Goldenberg Peanut Chews (another of the great contributions Jews made to our society), I got into an argument with two passing North-bounders on the relative merits of Maine versus Pennsylvania. One of them was from Maine, so I groused about the 278-mile trench of mud and moose moo. When he realized I was from Pennsylvania, he called it "The Podiatrist's Friend," saying the rocky trail almost crippled him.

"Maine," he said, "has a dry season. But no matter how strong the sun gets, it won't dry up those rocks. Besides, at least Maine has plenty of water to drink."

A few weeks later, here I am bruising my shins on those same rocks. For the first 140 miles in Pennsylvania, the AT follows the ridge atop the Blue Mountain, geologically one of the oldest ranges in the country. In place of rugged mountain peaks, the range has long flat stretches of broken rock, a last-ing tribute to the grinding forces of glaciers. Still, Pennsylvania has sweet water – one just has to look for it.

I finally arrived at "The Hilton on the AT" at 6:00 PM, the same time I originally planned, just three days later. I am writ-ing on a cable spool, which serves as the table. Miraculously, this spool encircles a living tree, a pretty neat trick indeed.

I ate by myself after a leisurely six-mile walk from the gap where I left for my free dinner at the camp. After the dental student came back from his exam, Mrs. Fluhr asked me to stay for the final ten days of camp as the co-counselor. Working at the camp would deliver a lot more good to a lot more people than my spending another ten days hiking, but I know once I stop for that long, I would not get going again. So, I said my goodbyes and walked back into the woods.

The "Hilton" was as grand as every Northbounder reported. The roof has translucent green Plexiglas panels that permits light to get through. Spring water pours out of a pipe and flows away from the site within a clever drainage system. Even the outhouse has class, with a half-moon cut out of its door and a Sear's catalogue next to the seat. This is the most beautiful and cleverest of settings, which is why we Thru-hikers call it, "The Hilton on the AT."

If the beauty of the six miles I walked from Swatara Gap continues, I have some fantastic hiking in store for me. Gone are the rock-strewn ridges, replaced by the gentle pathways through the Pennsylvania forest: they don't call this state Penn's Woods for nothing. I saw green all around me as I walk amongst ferns, laurel, and hemlock boughs. I passed creeks and springs for the first time since entering Pennsylvania. Here are the forests I last saw in New England and what rocks

I saw, sit amongst ferns, not filling the path. But there are more ridges ahead; I will not leave Blue Mountain for good until I reach the banks of the Susquehanna River.

Working at Eagle Springs typifies the spirit of the long-distance adventurer. Like Cooper's Natty Bumppo, I am alone and independent, but can drop in on civilization occasionally. My employment at Eagle Springs benefited my employers more than it did me. They needed me, whereas I slipped further behind the schedule I need to follow to avoid walking through those *"snow-peaked mountains way down south."* But no matter, I will think back fondly on my summer camp experience.

Even during the brief time I stayed at Eagle Springs, I felt I helped. Best of all, for a lonely Thru-hiker, the people there, both campers and counselors alike, included me in their conversions, their activities, as well as in their excursions to the Red Lion Inn, their favorite bar.

When I hike alone all day, I walk with a mind that flips between being filled with thoughts or cleared of thoughts. When cleared, I can notice all the details around me, from the different bark on the trees, the lichen covered granite, the darting movement of a salamander. Every step is filled with this beauty and interest. And yet, I cannot clear my head for long. I must slip into unconsciousness to avoid the monotony that comes from spending every day inside *the Long Green Tunnel.*

In our everyday life, we take for granted our ability to pick up a phone or walk next door to talk with someone. The past few days at camp have been like Mrs. Booz's mint iced tea for my mind; I could not get enough to quench my thirst and then, just like that, I am alone and thirsty again. Even the most inane conversations were joyful. For example, campers and counselors alike joined in the serious intellectual discussion about, if it were just a "three-hour tour," why did Ginger pack so many evening gowns? Important stuff.

Camps require close knit relationships to provide campers with a nurturing, safe environment. There can be no cracks through which the campers could fall. There can be friendly kidding, but nothing more, as the primary concern must be the health and welfare of the campers. The camp directors balanced providing a fun environment for staff, so that they stay the summer and come back, but also making sure the staff focuses on the campers. As I wandered around that first night, I could see from the direction of the counselors' eyes, they were aware of their charges. I could also tell they cared for each other. That showed in how quickly they covered for me when I pursued the mystery behind George's medication.

Once more in a co-ed environment, I felt pangs of loneliness. Frenchy expressed what I have been feeling for months. I miss companionship even more immediately after being around other people, than when I am completely alone, and I miss it a lot right now. This is why people can feel the loneliest in the middle of New York City on New Year's. I long for real connections with people. I want to hold hands with someone, have someone's head on my shoulder. I want to cook a meal with someone and then dine together. I long for a tender kiss and a warm embrace.

The girl counselors (with whom I failed to strike up even a short-term romance) will not be the only things I miss about the camp. I miss the intense discussions over the use of medications as a way of avoiding behaviors instead of dealing with people as they are. I will even miss the talks about backpacking. I will miss the feeling of altruism, working hard to make another human being feel special. Finally, I will miss a camp loaded with special people, each with his or her unique personality. So much can be done for our society if we view the campers as people who have the desire to contribute, rather than as "retards" or "handicapped," labels that make it easier to warehouse them in institutions and treat them as if they are not real people.

The people I met at Eagle Springs have different talents, but they do have talents, and they are more than willing to contribute. It is up to those of us who claim superior capabilities to apply of our gifts to help them uncover how they can best contribute, so that they can live within the rest of society. The idea of warehousing people, shutting them away in prisons of a different name, demonstrates the failure of our imagination, not theirs.

Camp Eagle Springs provides a ten-day oasis in the lives of these campers. The social and recreational activities exceeded those at any camp I have worked. The willingness to allow a counselor to challenge a prescribed dosage, proved their mission is the health and well-being of their charges. Many organizations would have quashed my dissent – especially coming from someone with a one-day history. My one complaint is the camp does not offer a nutritionally helpful diet. The campers get food they enjoy, but it is food high in sugar and low in protein. For example, today's breakfast consisted of pancakes and cold cereal. Yesterday's was an apple turnover, which everyone loved, but I know a thing or two about poor nutritional planning, a particular expertise of mine. If anyone wants a menu representing poor nutrition, I am your man. The food with the most protein they serve is peanut butter, again, closely resembling my menu planning. There is little roughage in the meals; three months of macaroni, Minute Rice, and instant mash potatoes have taught me the consequence of no fiber.

This morning, I amused several counselors when I slapped a toothless man on the back declaring, "Thanks, Harold, if it weren't for you, we'd all be eating steak and apples." He could have taken offense, but Harold cracked up at the jest.

CHAPTER THREE

Perseverance

AUGUST 27 AM.

Definitely Not "The Hilton on the AT"

I made another wrong choice.

I reached the Earl Shaffer Shelter around four yesterday. I could have reached the next Lean-to, Susquehanna Lean-to, probably in three hours, but that would have meant hanging around the next morning at the Lean-to, until Duncannon, the town across the Susquehanna River, woke up. I decided to purchase a tarp in the next town, because, as Eleanor Roosevelt might have said, "It is better to buy a tarp than curse the rain."

I spent yesterday hiking through the most beautiful section of the Pennsylvania Trail. Every mile, I passed another place where I would say, "Wow, what a great place to spend the night." Of course, what more can I say about where I spent the previous night?

The Lean-to at Rausch Gap is another of those places,

AT hikers tell each other about. With a flagstone patio and skylight, the Thruhikers have named it "The Hilton on the AT."

The Earl Shaffer Shelter, where I stayed last night, was the antithesis of the Hilton. Shaffer was a squat lean-to with a dirt floor -- and a huge boulder in the middle. Now what genius would build a Lean-to around a boulder? Perhaps Earl Shaffer ascended to heaven from that boulder. I let the three kids who got there before me sleep in the Lean-to; I slept under the stars. The guide book promised water a quarter mile away, not piped into the site itself; after all, how many "Hiltons" can there be? The water, it turned out, was not a quarter mile down the Trail, it was a quarter mile below the Trail. The kids said it took them forty minutes to go down and back.

"The hell with it," I said. My sole water jug was still mostly full. "This'll hold me until I reach the Susquehanna River." I ate dinner and read for several hours, drinking as little as possible.

What a shame to name such a bleak lean-to after the Jackie Robinson of the Appalachian Trail. Earl Shafer was the first person to hike the whole thing. When I think about the difficulty I faced with my boots, my pack, my food, and my water, I cannot imagine what he went through back in the 1940s. Since him, only about seventy people have officially hiked the whole thing – and gear and other logistics are the main causes for quitting. The other main causes are: will, desire, and meaning. And, of course, Chairback Mountain.

When I awoke the next morning, I took a swig of water and set off for the day's hike. There was, perhaps, another mouthful of water remaining in my container, but I felt certain I would find water before I reached the Susquehanna Shelter, seven miles away. The day got hot early. A fine layer of gray dust covered the bushes near the Trail. When I sipped the last of my water, I tried to hold it in my mouth for as long as possible.

When the mouth turns dry – really dry – not just the dryness that makes a person leave the TV for the fridge, things begin to go wrong. The tongue starts to fill the mouth. Breathing becomes a choking discomfort, as there is nothing left to swallow to keep the windpipe clear. But these things are physical. The mind begins to panic, taking steps towards fear. Somewhere, a quarter mile or so below the ridge line must be water. But the dense thicket covers treacherously sharp rocks with rattlesnakes hiding from the relentless heat of this August day. Nevertheless, collapsing from thirst might also be dangerous, and as the sun inched higher in the sky, that possibility loomed real.

During the first days after I entered Pennsylvania, I would load my mouth with blackberries, swirl my tongue around until my mouth filled with blackberry juice, then spent the next hour picking seeds out of my teeth. But after I took a week off in Philadelphia, and another three days at Camp Eagle Springs, the season for blackberries was behind us. The bushes turned brown and the fruit disappeared. Sumac, sassafras, black birch…. I went through the mental list of plants I could depend on for moisture. Nothing in sight. On I hiked, each step raising a tiny cloud of dust.

With no proof I would find water at the Susquehanna Shelter either, my only choice was to keep walking. When I reached the hard-paved Route 225 that crossed the ridge, still four miles away from the shelter, I hesitated at first, then walked down the road hoping to find a rest stop or roadside diner. But the heat radiating from the black asphalt made my head spin. My Vibram soles were sticking to the surface of the road; the steep downward slope pressed my toes against the front of my boots. Water or no water, I would last longer on the dirt Trail. I crossed to the other side of the road to return uphill to the Trail. When I reached the ridge, I looked down again and saw nothing but a black snakelike road, absorbing the full sun with no shade, with no place in view to find water.

The sun climbed higher in the sky. I became a soldier in the epic poem *Gunga Din*, willing to drink any type of water, whether it stunk of sulfur or crawled with wiggling mosquito larvae. I became apathetic. I was half way into a seven-mile hike and I could not bring myself to move. I thought, maybe I should turn around and head back to the Earl Shaffer shelter and drop down the side trail to fill my water bottle, at least I know there was water there. I kicked myself for not replacing the water bottles I lost along the way. A one quart container, 32 ounces of liquid for a 176-pound man, during August, is not enough to last a day, not when I am so far away from the sweet water of Maine.

Oh, how I missed Maine with its bubbling springs, its picturesque ponds, the cool, sweet water, there for the taking, as much as I wanted, whenever I wanted. And I loved the way the constant misting rain kept the dust from coating my tongue and filling my lungs.

I also took myself to task for not walking on after finding no water at the Earl Schaffer Lean-to. It was not as if I slept inside the shelter. Moreover, because an evening hike would have avoided the direct exposure to the sun, the remaining miles would not have treated me as harshly as they did the next day. Plus, my body would still have retained a nighttime's worth of water before my respiration released it while I slept. Since I slept under the sky anyway, I could have slept anywhere. An hour closer to Susquehanna last night, would have reduced my walking this morning. Why did I feel the need to sleep near that squat ugly shelter?

I know what it feels like to be thirsty. When I was twelve, my family spent a month camping on Mt. Desert Island, off the coast of Maine. We took a camping vacation every July. My dad used to say, "I can do twelve months' work in eleven, but I could never do twelve months' work in twelve."

My dad and I set off one day to climb Mt. Champlain. It is Cadillac Mountain, not Champlain, that is the highest mountain on the island and the highest point on the Atlantic coast north of Rio de Janeiro. Champlain is a VW bug compared to Cadillac Mountain, just over one thousand feet in elevation. Hiking the Precipice Trail to the top of Champlain did not seem like it would be that big a deal.

Because our canteens were the type that slung over the shoulder and flopped with each step – I owned my own by then – we left them with my mother, whom my dad asked to pick us up in the parking lot in three hours. One thousand feet; a three-hour tour; no big deal.

What we did not realize was that the one thousand feet would be straight up the side of a cliff. In some places, we climbed up ladders made of metal rungs, banged into the granite. Other times we inched along ledges or pulled ourselves over boulders. The sky was crystal blue and the sun seemed more than a thousand feet closer.

We came to a particularly long climb up the ladders. The topmost rung was smashed into the rock, perhaps from a falling boulder, so I thought. Reaching the next ledge meant reaching up to the stone ledge and clawing our way to it. I was not sure whether the trail went left or right, so I went straight and sat on the dirt until my father reached me. It became evident that the trail did not continue straight, since the slope ended at a rock wall. Nor did it go to the left. Someone made an "X" with two saplings, barring the way. No, the only way to go was to the right, for those climbing up the ladder. Having already gone straight, for us to reach the ledge to the right, we needed to jump over a gap to a thin ledge. Though the gap was just two feet, beyond the ledge, I looked out to infinity.

I froze.

Other hikers came up the ladder after us and we sent them the right way to the ledge. It then became obvious why there was no longer a top rung; the park rangers wanted us to go to the right in the first place, not scrape our way up to a ledge. If I led us to the right, instead of straight, I would have grasped a metal bar, put my foot on a granite step, and pulled myself onto the narrow ledge that wrapped itself along the granite wall. But I was so focused on looking up, I missed the now obvious clues, thus placing us in this predicament. I sat there trying to calm my rising panic and fight my growing thirst. I was having difficulty swallowing. Fatigue may make cowards of us all, but thirst makes us stupid. My one hope was that those clever park rangers, anticipating all this, would place one of those red Coca Cola coolers, filled with bottles of ice cold soda, at the top of the mountain. But first, we needed to jump the gap to the narrow ledge.

We were in a quandary. I could see my father was not keen to jump to the tiny ledge with the long drop behind it. Yet we sat on an open rock face on the side of the mountain, facing the full brunt of the summer sun on our heads and faces – and feeling very thirsty.

How long we sat on that ledge – I do not know. It seemed like a long time. Several groups passed us, each benefitting from our example of what not to do. Finally, my father slid on his stomach off the ledge, into the unknown. His legs found the lower rungs of the ladder and he grabbed the top rung before slipping off. He went down another rung, then back up, this time climbing to the right, my left. Grasping the chain that was bolted to the granite wall, he reached his hand out to me and we linked arms. On the count of three, I jumped off the ledge and my father swung me through space until my feet landed on the ledge. Holding onto the metal rods hammered into the granite, we inched forward.

In about two minutes, we pulled ourselves to the top of the mountain. There was no soda cooler; not even a water fountain. Instead, there was a gradual slope that led us to the road in ten minutes. From there we walked along the road toward the parking lot where we started. We could see a familiar car racing up the road. My mother passed us, turned around, and drove up beside us. When we failed to show at the parking lot at the appointed time, she frantically drove up and down the road looking for us. We got in, telling her of the mishap, while we drank the warm water from the canteens we left behind.

It was the memory of that mountain ledge that kept me from going with my Dad and the rest of the Boy Scout troop to Philmont when I turned fifteen. I could not see the point of spending ten days walking in the desert, regardless of how many people assured me the reservation is not the barren dessert I imagined.

I thought back on that terrific thirst, as I walked without water to the Susquehanna River. I knew there would be no red Coca Cola cooler at the Susquehanna Lean-to, but certainly hoped the Trail planners would place this lean-to close to drinkable water. My only choice was to keep moving, despite the effort it took to raise and lower my legs.

The faster I walked, the more water I expired; the slower I walked, the more likely I would shrivel up like a raisin in the sun. If left to my subconscious, I would have walked off the ridge, sat under a tree, and waited until someone brought me a mint ice tea. I was hot, tired, and thirsty; walking fast in the hot sun with a backpack is not what the body wants to do under these conditions. I came to a power line clearing. If I walked down the grassy slope, I would surely find water, but then again, I might not. I stopped for a moment to rest with my pack off. The air cooled my back, which was damp with sweat. I breathed easier without the strain.

I looked at my pack. If I leave it on the ridge, I would reach Susquehanna faster. I could find water, satisfy my thirst, and reclimb the ridge to retrieve my pack. Thirst makes us stupid, but the power of the subconscious, the same subconscious that kept me plastered to that ledge on Mt. Champlain, was moments away from taking control. I would weaken unless I found moisture.

That was when I spied them: the last blackberries of the season. Three plump berries hanging on a bush, picked by neither man nor beast.

I held the blackberries in my hand, as I walked the last miles to the shelter. Every few minutes, I would eat another blackberry corpuscle, carefully rationing the precious drops of moisture. The tiny amount of

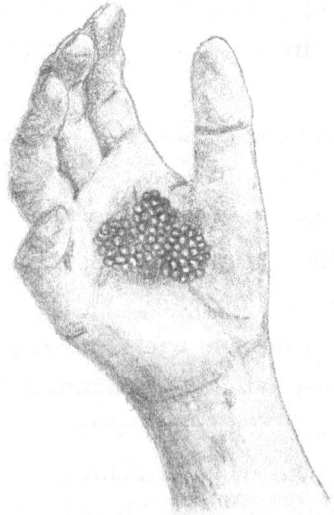

juice in each cell did not quench my thirst, but it kept me going. I moved quickly, lest my berries ran out before my miles did.

I have worked under strain before, beyond my limits. When I rowed for the college crew team, when each of us was already pulling with all our strength, the coxswain would yell out, "Power Ten!" and we would pull even harder for the count of ten. We were already pulling as hard as we could but the shouts of the coxswain would somehow coax even more out of our straining limbs. Whenever I ate a berry bubble, I shouted, "Power Ten!" On and off again, I bit into the blackberry then took ten powerful long strides, almost at a trot. I hiked to an invisible coxswain. Whenever my pace slowed, I would pop a blackberry bubble, and shout for another "Power Ten."

At long last, the trail sloped downwards toward the Susquehanna, marking the end of the Blue Mountain in Pennsylvania. The sky was turning dark and the sun, which beat on me all morning, began to slip behind clouds. After an entire night, and a seven mile walk on just a few mouthfuls of water, I finally reached the Susquehanna Shelter. As I approached, I heard a rushing stream. The first drops of rain were already falling when I laid my pack in the shelter and took my cup and jug to fill in the stream.

Water at last. How sweet it tasted. How good it felt. I drank and drank from my Sierra cup while lightening crackled above the ridge. Then I returned to the shelter to wait out the storm.

AUGUST 27 PM.

Skill or Just Luck

I would rather be lucky than smart. With my knowledge of the outdoors, I squeezed out of many a tight spot; but whenever

Lady Luck moves her chips to some other square, my skills are as worthless as crossed fingers at a crap table.

I cannot remember how many times I said, "That branch ought to hold me," before falling into an onrushing stream. Nor can I recall all the pieces of equipment I lost after securing them to my pack with the best knots an Eagle Scout can tie. Something always monkeys up the works. That is why I believe there is a mysterious ingredient at work beyond our control.

I thought about this as I walked along the macadam road south of Duncannon, Pennsylvania. Duncannon is the town just west of the Susquehanna River, where the Trail turns south after crossing half of Pennsylvania in a westerly, boot-eating, ankle-twisting, thirst-inducing, direction. Good old, wet, muddy Maine – how I miss it. Duncannon is not much of a town, but I spent a considerable amount of my morning there. I bought a large piece of clear plastic and asked the proprietor of the hardware store to hammer three grommets into either side. He was nice enough to do it and only charged me for the price of the grommets and the plastic – and the new canteen. From now on, when I need to camp in the rain, I will have a ceiling that will be large enough to keep me and my belongings dry. I left my pack with the proprietor and bought a tuna sandwich and a Sprite from a nearby luncheonette.

When I was ten, I would take the Pennsylvania Railroad to downtown Philadelphia one day a week so I could attend a class at the Academy of Natural Sciences. What I remember most from the experience was eating lunch in the underground concourse of Suburban Station. After a few Saturdays, I would sit down and, without asking, the waitress brought me a tuna fish sandwich on toast with a glass of Sprite. Duncannon brought back the memory of someone looking out for me.

With my luck, having now built my portable shelter, it will probably not rain again. This is like a game of chess. I make a move and my opponent makes a move. I leave my umbrella in the car; it rains. I take my umbrella with me; it does not rain. But it is not God toying with me; what am I to God that he would move to thwart me? It is just randomness combined with a situational memory. We may walk on the crack a thousand times, but we only remember that one time our mother's back actually broke.

Does God determine when the buttered side of a slice of bread lands face down or is that just a bad outcome in a string of random occurrences? Or do we conveniently fail to recall the equal number of times we avoided a negative outcome. We eat the bread if it lands butter-side up (provided less than three seconds have lapsed) and then quickly forget about it; after all, what is the big deal about eating a slice of bread. Yet, having to throw out a slice of buttered bread now covered with dog hair and unidentified shiny particles, makes that outcome the more exceptionable and, hence, the more memorable.

It is late August and the thunderstorm season may have ended in Pennsylvania. That is weather, not God. Have we created God in our own image as a meddler who enjoys annoying his flock? My relationship with God is neither one of fear nor transaction. I do not make promises for favors and I do not worry that God is punishing me. If a duck eats the bread crumbs I leave behind, I blame the duck, not God. If, like Odysseus, who claimed too much of the success for defeating the Trojans, I come across like an arrogant jerk, my punishment will not come from God, but from my fellow men, who have a way of dealing with arrogant jerks. I believe that when we look to God to fix the problems of the world, God looks back at us and says, "I created you to fix the problems. That was my miracle."

We have to fix ourselves and then we have to fix the problems of our own creation, especially those we created in the name of faith. So a religion tells its faithful they will ascend to heaven if they suspend the gift of reason to rely on faith alone. If you have to rely on faith, it means your intelligence rejects what you see or think. If you reject reason for faith, are you saying God gave you the ability to reason between right and wrong, but now you know better than God? Why would you turn off that part of your brain? Why did God give you reason if you then refuse to use it? Unquestioned religious faith is like any devotion to a mob, it relies on suspending the responsibility of your own actions in subservience to the group. That is not something to be proud of.

After collecting my pack and rain shelter, I headed south to find the Trail. The main street of Duncannon gave way to gravel filled lots and ramshackle buildings. I was taking this street south hoping it would intersect the Trail, which I left north of town in search of the hardware store. After walking in the hot afternoon sun on concrete and tarmac, I saw a single white blaze on a tree. On I walked, figuring I joined the Trail. After a while, I snapped out of my daze, realizing that I knew not the faintest idea which way to turn. I knew the Trail changed directions, because I just saw two rectangular white blazes, one on top of the other, on a nearby oak. Unfortunately, there were no other blazes in sight. I flipped through my guidebook, but it was of no use. I was on a part of the Trail the local hiking club relocated after the publication of the Pennsylvania guidebook I carried.

I could do little more than search aimlessly for the next blaze. I figured the Trail ran to the right, southwest, away from Duncannon, but after walking a few minutes, I drew a blank. I returned to the oak tree and set off in the other direction – still no blaze. A car approached from the south. I flagged it down with my hat.

"I'm a little misplaced, sir, and I was wondering if you've seen a white blaze on a tree anywhere?"

"You hiking the Appalachian Trail?"

"Yes, sir."

"Why didn't you say so? There is a marker back-a-way... why don't you get yourself a guidebook?"

Notice I only admitted to being misplaced, not lost – a distinction I learned from Daniel Boone, played by Fes Parker in the Disney version. He would never say he was lost, because lost implies not knowing where you are, whereas misplaced means you know where you are and you know where you want to go; you just haven't quite reckoned how to make the two meet.

The driver was right. I walked down the highway just a few yards to find a wooden marker pointing to a clearly marked path to the left. Once back on the Trail, the guidebook told me to look for a jeep road that would lead me one and a half miles to the Darlington Lean-to, where I intended to spend the night. But with so many changes, how could I know I was on the same path as described in the guidebook? I may be on the jeep road or I might be on some other path. There could be more than one jeep road or the Trail Club could have abandoned the jeep road, with the idea of taking us Thruhikers in a new, more scenic, direction. I was in no mood to futz around; I was a long way from the Earl Shaffer lean-to, where I started my day, desperate for water. I wanted to take off my boots, soak my feet, eat dinner, and pass out. One and a-half-miles should take me less than thirty minutes if the terrain worked in my favor. I took a deep breath, hitched up my pack, and set off – almost missing the 3 x 5 card tacked to a tree that signaled yet another Trail relocation. On the card was the drawing of an arrow, no words, no other identification, pointing straight up the slope.

I looked up the trail – it was steep. I trained to hike the Appalachian Trail by carrying a pack loaded with books up a hill to an observatory near where I lived in college. I likened those climbs to Kip Keino's daily runs up Agony Hill as he trained for the Olympics; I always was one for self-delusion. Nevertheless, a night's rest waited for me up the steep incline, so I took another deep breath, re-hitched my pack, and started climbing. I kept my focus on the ground, lest I stumble on the rocky terrain. I scrambled up the steep embankment. With a burst of energy, I got past the steep part of the climb. When I reached the top. I had to stop to catch my breath and to look behind at the steep path I just climbed. Before me I saw a narrow dirt road leading along the crest of the ridge. This must be the jeep road, I thought.

After walking for about one hundred yards, I noticed there were no blazes in sight. I remembered seeing blazes when I left the road, but now on top, I could see none. All of the AT training warns that when you cannot find a blaze, turn around and walk back until you find one. But I hate to give up ground I just climbed and that hill was too steep to risk climbing again. I figured that, just like before, a blaze would turn up. Besides, the hill was steep.

I walked on, dreaming of one thing or another. I remembered driving back to Philly last New Year's Day from a bunch of parties near Washington. That morning, I attended a brunch at the home of Rob Perry, a college friend from Alexandria. By the time I hit the road, it was afternoon. An hour into the drive, the combination of the monotony of I-95 and the fatigue of the previous twenty-four hours caught up with me and I began to feel drowsy. My solution, in my dopey subconscious, was to rest no more than one side of my brain at a time, first closing one eye, then another, trying to nap with half my body for fifteen seconds at a time. But surprisingly this did not restore me. So then I tried closing both eyes for five seconds at a time, popping my eyes open in time to steer the car back between the lines. Fortunately, from deep inside my brain, a parent seeped through the gelatin to order me off the road to take a nap. Why can't these parents just leave us alone and let us live our own lives?

I was beginning to feel that same drowsiness again. The combination of the August heat, the extremely long day, the stress of my dash to the Susquehanna desperately seeking water, took its toll. Normally, walking requires no thought; the subconscious mind triggers the muscles to move. But when the subconscious wants to put my body to sleep, I must consciously direct my legs to lift and fall.

Grass grew on the jeep road, which evidently was not used much. There was a rusted barbed wire fence in some places and on every few trees hung "No Hunting Signs." Every hundred yards or so, I could see what appeared to be a faded white blaze haphazardly slapped on a tree.

So the blazes weren't perfect; am I so perfect? Are any of us perfect? Besides, these blazes gave me trouble all day. I noticed my shadow in front of me. I tried walking up my shadow but whenever I quickened my pace, the shadow moved faster in front of me. That pretty much describes my life. I am forever trying to catch my shadow, walking to the horizon, without noticing what I am passing along the way.

After some more time – I lost hold of how much time passed – I noticed the path became more overgrown and occasionally trees grew right in the middle of the jeep road. I began having second thoughts about the blazes, which I no longer could find. I cursed myself for not turning around earlier; but since I walked this far, I kept walking, figuring the jeep road would have to lead somewhere.

My shadow grew longer as the setting sun glowed over my shoulder.

Usually, as I hike, I am alert, but deep in thought. That is how I have come up with so many solutions to the troubles facing mankind. Of course, I tend to forget most of them by the time I write them down. But this day was different. With so much heat and humidity, and the dehydration from the morning, I did not have the thought process capable of a quick solution; I kept staring at my lengthening shadow.

"Think," a voice came from inside my addled head. "If it is late in the day and I am walking up my shadow, then –?"

Finally, I figured it out. If the sun sets in the west, and I am walking up my shadow, I must be walking east, the opposite of the direction the Trail takes on the western side of the Susquehanna River. Not only was I not on the Trail, but no matter how far I walked, I would never hit the Appalachian Trail; I would, however, eventually reach, and subsequently drown, in the Susquehanna River. I put my pack down and pulled out my map and compass. This old jeep trail, or whatever it was that I was on, did not appear on the map. Then the second revelation dawned on me. This was no road at all. It was the border of the

Pennsylvania State Game Land, which would explain all the "No Hunting" signs.

I should have turned around and obeyed the guidebook an hour ago, and gone back to find the last blaze. But by the time I realized I was heading in the wrong direction, it was late, and I could not envision a future spent wandering back and forth in the vicinity of Duncannon. Some rules were made to be broken and some rules merely express the natural order of the world, the accrued wisdom of the ages. Turning around and walking back until finding the last confirmed blaze, then turning back around to follow the true Trail, even if it meant climbing down and then up the very ridge I labored to climb, even if it meant returning to the hard-paved road where I first lost the blazes – these were rules established by tradition, the rules of man. But if I followed these pedantic rules, I might as well camp by the side of the highway because, as it was getting late and the sun was setting, I would not be able to reenter the forest and see the blazes well enough to follow them to the Darlington Shelter; after all, I was not able to find these blazes in daylight; I certainly would not find them at night.

I really want to reach Georgia before I die, so I can end this unwelcome and unsought-after trek. Walking back and forth over the same section of trail was not going to restore my life. Not even Steve Jackson can reach Georgia by hiking north (well, maybe with a dogsled and some space age plastic). So instead of heading back to the road, I oriented my compass to the southwest to find the hypotenuse of the triangle formed by the true Trail on my map and the easterly direction I just traveled. The unknown factor, the length of this hypotenuse, would depend on how far I just walked in the wrong direction.

Walking along the hypotenuse, I figured, would mean I

would hike through uncharted woods, off any type of path. I would need to employ the dead reckoning skills I learned in my Orienteering Merit Badge. First, I would set my compass in the direction I wish to follow and then locate two landmarks along the same line. When I reach the first, I would look at the second landmark, raise my compass within eyesight so I could run an imaginary line from the directional arrow through the first landmark to find a farther landmark along the same line. That way, I can hike in a straight line, even without a path. That's how it worked in the merit badge book.

I figured I would reach either the Appalachian Trail or the Darlington trail, an orange blazed trail that crosses the AT near the Darlington Shelter. But to do this required I take a few risks. First, since I did not know where on the map I stood, dead reckoning could take hours and it was already late in the day. Second, it would mean leaving the smooth, grassy, unmarked jeep road, or whatever it was I just followed, to cut through the unknown forest, with whatever obstacles lay in store. And finally, when I successfully completed the merit badge six years ago, we practiced our dead reckoning in an open field, with wooden stakes hammered in the ground. Now, this gets real.

Hiking along a trail marked by white blazes all of a sudden became tame. I followed a path for three months, something laid out with forethought and well-trod, in both directions, by countless others. But at this point, I was about to wander into the unknown, hoping to intersect one or more trails that could lie any number of miles away from where I stood, since I did not know where I stood. My instinct proved wrong already about the jeep trail. Are the odds now going to revert in my favor or does each risk I take assume the same odds? Am I on an unlucky streak? I looked back from the direction I came and then took off in the direction my compass pointed.

After a few steps, I descended steeply from the ridge. What do you know? I climbed the wrong ridge. I hiked through the woods for a while, heedless of any danger to myself. If I broke my leg, nobody would find me. I thought about the tablets of morphine my doctor gave me for just this situation. Once in the swale below the ridge, I could no longer see the sun. There was not even a hint of a path or road. I climbed over rocks and fallen trees. The rocks were covered with moss and the bark of the fallen trees was damp and slick. The going was very slow.

I was losing steam. What promised to be a brisk hike up a jeep road, turned into a two-and-a-half-hour test of my endurance. When I reached for my new canteen, I found it was empty. For the second time in the same day, I became extremely thirsty. Even if there were blackberries around, it was too dark to find them.

What's worse, I wasn't really following the dead reckoning, because the forest was so dark, I could not see a second land-mark. I could not judge whether I headed straight along the hypotenuse, or I was zigging and zagging.

I walked on, looking for either the white blazes of the Appalachian Trail or water, ready to camp at the first sign of either. It was night and under the trees I could use neither the moon nor the stars to light the way. I switched on my flashlight to make sure I kept my bearings southwest; forget the idea of keeping two points in sight – I could barely see my compass.

Then I stepped on to a grassy path leading due west. I abandoned my previous plan and turned onto this path, not knowing where it might lead, but at least, the path was clear of roots and rocks. I thought of my night walking in New Jersey when

I nearly stepped on the rattlesnake. I was thirsty that night too and recalled thinking snake meat might provide moisture. I walked through trickling water flowing across the path at the bottom of a hollow. The water glistened in the tiny beam of my mini flashlight as it crossed the muddy road – but it was water. A frightened woodchuck scurried into the thicket at my approach. Sloshing into the water I tried to decide whether to drink it, untreated or not.

Dysentery aside, I was all set to fill my Sierra Cup with the water when the tiny beam of my flashlight reflected upon a pile of rubbish. What a thrill. An Honest-to-God pile of beer cans, boots, and tires. What a sight for my tired, thirsty eyes.

"Now, who in their right mind," I said to the woodchuck, "Would leave all that junk out here in the middle of nowhere?"

I hoped his answer would have been: "No one; because we are not in the middle of nowhere."

In a few yards, his words proved correct. There it was: a path wide enough to drive a jeep on, complete with rectangular white blazes in both directions. I found the Appalachian Trail. With one last look at my compass, I turned south along this level, well-marked jeep road, and within a few minutes descended into a hollow where I came upon the Darlington Shelter. Fifteen minutes later, here I am sitting at the picnic table, writing under the light of my candle lantern, cooking my dinner on my Svea stove, with my Sierra cup filled with sweet cold water.

Like I said: "When you're lucky, who needs skill?"

AUGUST 30.

Sour Grapes

I came upon an unexpected pleasure called Fuller Lake, at the Pine Grove Furnace State Park in Pennsylvania. Once, long ago, hydraulic pumps toiled to remove the water from this iron ore quarry, but with the pumps silenced, the pit has filled with water.

Hiking through the Cumberland Valley covered me with a layer of humid grime. I was thinking only a razor would get me clean – a body shave – but a long soak in Fuller Lake did the job. It helped my psyche too. Between the warm rays of the sun and the gentle currents of the water I felt like I was getting a massage. I almost dozed off floating on my back, although every so often, I passed through water so chilling it woke me from my daze with a shudder. Fingers of cold stretched from the depths of the old iron ore pit: teeth chattering, bone aching, cold. After the last few days of thirst and heat, I tried to memorize the sensation this chill created on my body.

Once finished with my swim, I pretended to be a normal vacationer. I played Frisbee with some kids, chatted with a young couple, and was even able to pet a golden retriever, who, true to his name brought me a ball to throw, so he could retrieve. He was not full grown, but his big paws indicated that when done, he would be the size of a lion. No matter how far I threw the ball, he brought it back, dropping it at my feet. He would stare at it, look me in my eyes, and then draw my gaze back to the ball.

"You want me to throw the ball." He looked up at me, then down at the ball.

"Okay, let's under-
stand this. You are bringing me the ball thinking
I have no choice but to
throw it, because that is
what you think I'm bred
to do. You think I can't
help myself. You think
I can't resist throwing
your stupid ball. Is that
the game; is that what
you think of me?" I
threw the ball. Boy, did
he have me pegged.

The smell of charcoal filled the air with a sweet, smoky
fragrance. Like Charlie Brown, I never enjoy a hot dog as much
as when I watch a baseball game, but in my protein starved
condition, it took all my will power not to walk over and grab
the roasting meat right off the grill.

I sat propped against a tree and tried to read, enjoying the
clean feeling for the first time in a week. I watched as a young
couple on a blanket played with their baby boy. I am not ready
to feed, change, and stay up nights with a baby, but when I
watch these two, not much older than myself, I witness a magi-
cal transformation from self-absorbed kids into parents, willing to do anything for the little stranger who intruded upon
their lives. Not that I was counting, but they kissed him well
in excess of five hundred times, just while I was sitting there. I
suppose I can rationally understand the work and expense of a
baby, but the pleasure parents receive must be something that
cannot be so easily distilled into words and numbers.

I watched the family with the golden retriever leave for their car. They carried their picnic basket, blanket, and aluminum folding chairs from the clearing to the graveled parking lot. About halfway there, the big golden dog bolted back to where they picnicked, searched for a moment, his fluffy long tail waving back and forth enthusiastically, until he found what he was looking for. He ran back to the car with the tattered felt cover of what was once a tennis ball.

As people started to pack up and leave, I slung on my pack and left the picnic area. I read in the trail guide that a country store was just a short walk down the road and I planned to buy some chicken or a steak. After smelling the sweet smoky air given off by the charcoal grills, I yearned for grilled meat, a baked potato, maybe a salad with vinaigrette, some Gorgonzola cheese crumbled on top, along with chopped tomato and onion. Maybe, I could find some Pillsbury Crescent Rolls and cook them on a flat rock by my fire. And, of course, a cold beer would go down well about then.

I have hit a lot of country stores along the way. I thought about the little stores in Maine that advertised, "We sell Italians." Thinking this was some form of slavery, I valiantly charged the redoubt, but it turned out they were selling Italian sandwiches, or, as we say down Philly, "Hoagies." Like Lincoln before me, I emancipated as many as I could.

No sooner did I see the store, when this couple, the Grants, stopped me to chat. They were walking what appeared to be a dog, for I assume people do not walk their guinea pig.

The Grants knew many of the places I visited. I told them how just that morning, while hiking on a six-inch wide trail that ran along the Conodoguinet Creek, I kept to those six inches because of the dense poison ivy crowding either side, I came face-to-face with a fox. (Actually, it was more like knee-to-face.) Considering neither he nor I wished to step into the poison ivy, and since I was more curious about him than he was of me, he turned around and officially became a Southbounder. For the next half mile, he trotted in front of me, furtively glancing over his shoulder, no doubt wishing I would give it a rest. At the point where the Trail crossed the creek, he ducked under the bridge and then, once I passed, I suppose he resumed his Northbound trot.

As I walked, I recalled the time a fox wandered behind the houses on my street – so we called Animal Control. They sent this skinny guy with a wide brimmed Smokey Bear hat. We thought he would set a trap, but instead, he warned us to go back into our houses. We tried to see what he was doing through the kitchen window. Suddenly, we heard a "bang!" Holy mackerel! He shot the little fox, no doubt splattering its brains over the driveway. Then came another "bang!" followed by a third and a fourth. The way he was firing, he would soon need to reload. We called about a fox and they sent us "Elmer Fudd."

The Grants were so good an audience I lost track of time. I excused myself and hustled down the road to the store, but was too late. The store closed at half past five. I settled for a Fresca from the soda machine on the front porch; it looked like another night of instant mashed potatoes and beef jerky for me.

The Grants strolled by the store and saw I lost my race with time.

"Good," said Mrs. Grant, "Now you must dine with us." Well, what was I supposed to do, argue?

A pot of chicken curry simmered on the stove, which we ate over rice. They served rolls and a salad – all of which I washed down with a few cold bottles of Molson beer. We sat around on the back porch and talked about history, about places we visited – they have seen a lot more than I – and the merits of Single Malt Scotch, a whole new world for me. It was a wonderful evening.

Over dinner, Dr. Grant explained curry to me. He said, "A chicken curry should be hot enough to cause beads of sweat to form on one's brow, but not so hot as to make them run." Having been born in England, where Indian food was part of his culinary tradition, he appreciated all manners of well prepared food, but, as Mrs. Grant chided, not enough to prepare any of it himself.

Their little dog, whom they called Keezle, named after what, I never learned, is a terrier mix – with one ear standing up and the other flopping down. His eyes were disproportionately large for his face. It took a few seconds for him to decide if I were all right. After that, he sat in my lap after dinner, looking up into my face, much like a furry baby.

After a long hot shower, I fell asleep under a feather comforter. I was slow to leave the next morning: where did I have to go in such a hurry? While we ate scrambled eggs with homemade smoked trout, we watched two deer stroll past the back porch in even less of a hurry than I.

I felt better for staying with the Grants and when I finally left, I took on a whole new attitude. I am a Thruhiker, bound for Georgia, carrying the well wishes of such wonderful people as the Grants, who will stay behind in their lovely cottage, taking hot showers, sleeping under feather comforters, drinking cold Molson and sipping single malt scotch, while I walk, day after day, through the sweltering late-August heat.

Thanks to a good night's rest, I found my first decent pace in days. Has there ever been a greater joy? With a good pace, the hiker does not think about time, distance, or blisters. Walking becomes as natural as breathing.

I hiked past what looked like a ruined village with a huge barn. The guidebook says the Civilian Conservation Corps camped there during the Great Depression, building many of the huts and paths in this section of the Trail. A few years later, the Navy kept captured German U-boat crews there. Little remains of the buildings, but grape vines hung over the Trail.

Although on the sour-side, they offered the grape-within-a-grape consistency of a Concord grape.

Increasingly, it is not the beauty of the Trail that I am noting in my journal, but my interactions with people. I am walking south, not because there is anything I hope to see that is any better than what I have already seen, not because I am walking for a cause, but because I do not know how to stop walking. I suppose when I reach Springer Mountain, I will know I accomplished something special. I will be able to stroll up to women and say, "Hey there, baby, I hiked the Appalachian Trail (with the exception of a few miles at the beginning of New Hampshire and seventeen miles in Connecticut, and roughly five miles in New Jersey, although percentage-wise, that still rounds up close to 100%). And yet, when I finish hiking in another two months, I may very well find that besides solitude, I accomplished nothing that will benefit my future nor anyone else's either.

If I spend the next two months working on a scientific discovery, that would be significant. Of course, there is no guarantee I would discover anything, at least I could say I endeavored to do something for the betterment of humanity; for me, hiking to Georgia, does not.

Researchers stand their ground in the face of criticism and carry on despite the odds. Anything of any good comes from people willing to buck the trend, to do what others would leave undone. Do I need the approval of others to accomplish something of value or can I find the truth in what I do? I can walk forever if I can figure out who that would help, even if the person it helps is me. I thought hiking would, at least, get me into great shape, but it has shifted all my muscle to my legs, leaving my arms weaken and my chest sunken.

I thought the hike would reveal my future, but all it taught is I can suffer a lot more pain and discomfort than I ever imagined. As for my future, I am not a step closer to knowing where my life will lead. I know my father takes vicarious pleasure from my hike and I want to live up to him. At my age, he already served in the Navy during one war and would serve again as an officer during the next. I also feel I owe him one. When he was our scoutmaster, he took the troop to Philmont, the high adventure camp in New Mexico. All I could think of was walking through the desert, dying of thirst. I did not go, instead I worked that summer at a day camp. I need to show him I am not afraid of a challenge.

After the grapes, I hiked the remainder of the day along smooth trails until I reached Caledonia State Park, where I swam in "a cement pond," a real swimming pool. I leaned my pack against the fence so I could keep an eye on it, stripped to my shorts (which meant taking off my boots and socks) then plunged in. I figured I would swim twenty or thirty laps for starters, then hit the diving board. But when after ten minutes of swimming and not reaching mid pool, I switched to Esther Williams style water ballet and just stayed wet. I guess I have rebuilt myself for hiking and not much else. My huge, over developed legs are no longer buoyant, while my tiny T-Rex arms do not pull me through the water.

Having emerged well cleaned for a second day in a row, I decided to see a play at the nearby Maureen Stapleton Playhouse. Although I saw *The Crucible* once before, I went anyway, just to fit in with the crowd. I made some curried Minute Rice with canned shrimp, then hid my pack under a picnic table. The curry powder lacked the heat to cause beads of sweat to form on my brow, so it would not have passed Dr. Grant's test.

The picnic table was under the bough of a huge sycamore tree, so I would know where to find my pack later in the dark. After the show, I hung around the lobby, ready to discuss plot and characterization, in hopes a nice couple would invite me back to their cedar cottage. I would even join them for a second dinner: I am just that kind of guy. Finally, when the theater manager began turning out the lights, I went back to my pack, unrolled my sleeping bag on the picnic table, and fell asleep.

For a whole day and a half, I enjoyed myself in the company of others. The weather may have been hot and humid, but the swims washed the grime away. Nevertheless, something was lost. Passing all those people, but walking alone; doing things half-way, like seeing a play without anyone to discuss it with afterwards; coming to fun places, but leaving before I could really enjoy them – has made me feel apart from everyone else. What am I doing? I wondered if even those U-boat crews felt more at home. They could at least stick around until the grapes turned sweet.

CHAPTER FOUR

Common Sense

SEPTEMBER 1.

A Foolish Consistency

I think it was Emerson who said, "Only dead men and fools never change their minds."

But then Willie Mays, countered, "Winners never quit and quitters never win."

So, what would it be? To hike or not to hike? The empty feeling that comes from pursuing a false dream robs me of the strength to hike during the day and the peace to sleep well at night.

I hiked just six miles yesterday before hitching to the village of Gettysburg, where I took the tour of the battlefield, visited museums, and bought food – lots of food. I planned to sleep on the battlefield, but after the interpretive lectures and slide shows, I no longer wished to share the hallowed ground with the thousands who died there. I walked two miles south to a private campground where I showered, called home, and then slept under the stars. My phone call cheered no one, as I described, with no enthusiasm, how I spent the day not hiking.

I left the Trail from a place called Mont Alto, but instead of returning there, I completed the triangle by hitching farther south to Frederick, Maryland. My thoughts were torn between the guilt I was feeling for avoiding thirty miles of hiking, and my desperation, because I knew I would have to return to the Trail. What would be the point of hitching to Springer Mountain? Heading south only makes sense if I walk.

But why walk? I no longer saw the point of it. Okay. I left Maine not knowing what I wanted to do for the rest of my life and so I thought some break from the normal routine would help sort things out. I have since realized, that life is like the Trail; I need to just put one foot in front of the other. Or maybe life is like a mountain. Sometimes we can't see the peak from the base, but we start climbing anyway. Good things will either come or they won't, but I will never get anywhere in life staying in my sleeping bag saying "Ciao" – I get that point already. One must actually move to get anywhere.

If only I could summon the courage to leave the Trail for good. When my hiking partner asked me to help him achieve his dream, I may be the only person who interpreted that to mean I was obligated to walk the entire Trail – all 2,147 miles of it. All he asked me to do was help him achieve his dream; I did that. I got him to Maine and we parted ways in Connecticut. I satisfied my debt five states ago.

For myself, my goal was to do something different with my life, so I could maybe figure out how to become a man. Now, I am afraid to stop hiking, lest people call me a quitter. And yet, by staying on the Trail, I am acting like a marionette to my fears, which hardly seems to make me much of a man.

Everyone I pass wishes me luck and praises my accomplishment of having walked from Maine. But I tell myself that all the praise disappears if I do not make it to Georgia.

I spent the day in a pizza shop reading and drinking beer. A person reading a book in a pizza shop already looks out of place, but add to that the red hat, the scraggly beard, and the huge blue pack – strange doesn't even begin to describe it. Later, I walked over to the movie theatre and watched a film about a college basketball player (played by the brilliant Robby Benson) who finally realized that he no more controlled the ball, than it did him. He sacrificed his life because of his dream, a dream that changed long before he finally realized it. He quit the game to take control of his life.

Outside the theater, a fellow with long hair and a beard approached me. At first, I thought he was trying to sell me drugs, but then I remembered, my hair is also long and I sport a beard too. I wondered if people react to me based on my scraggly looks, which may explain why I stood alone in the lobby of the theatre after that play. Without my pack, I am just some scraggly looking man: a hippy, a bum. I get invited places when I am with my pack, because I capture the longing of all those who dream of doing something adventurous. I proved, once again, I am just as shallow.

He offered to drive me back to the Trail, many miles out of his way. Although I appreciated the lift, his need to give it made me wonder. So many people have encouraged me. Why? Were they just being nice or were they living vicariously through me on the Trail? People seem to do things for me as if I were cast into the wilderness to atone for their sins. Some gave me their address so I could send them a card when I finished; people I met for all of five minutes. Why are they doing this?

In Maine, I told everyone I was Georgia-bound. By Pennsylvania, people told me I was Georgia-bound. That is not where the motivation must come to get the feet moving in the morning.

There is a story in Appalachian Trail lore about the first woman who hiked the whole trail. She was ill equipped and poorly trained, a frail grandmother, but she was driven with a burning passion to hike the Appalachian Trail and to get the hell out of her marriage. Then there is me: a comparatively well-equipped and excellently trained young man, in superb physical condition. The difference? She followed her dream, whereas I followed someone else's dream.

Jeff, the scraggly man, dropped me in front of a tavern, near where he thought the Trail crossed the highway. We shook hands and he said, "I wish I was hiking with you." I looked longingly at his car as he drove away in the direction he came. "I wish I was driving east with you."

I figured I would sleep on the Trail once I found it. But where along the unlit Route 40 did the Trail cross, to the east or west? Driving west to the tavern, we did not see a sign or a blaze, but it was so dark, we could have missed the sign, if there was one. Besides, the AT does not always cross over mountain highways; sometimes it cuts under them through a culvert or under a bridge. Since it was dark and late, I walked into the tavern to ask for directions.

"Mountain Man!"

The tavern was filled with construction workers from a nearby pipe-line project. A loud, sandy-haired fellow with a mustache, beckoned me to the bar. I swung off my pack, letting it down carefully, pantomiming for any would-be pack thieves that it would be too heavy to casually whisk away. I walked to the bar where this fellow, John, already ordered me a beer.

I found myself telling stories of the fun and adventure of the Trail, like the time I stood nose-to-nose with this giant of a teenage moose. As beer followed beer, I forgot my emptiness for a while. We played several rounds of pool, with me actually winning a couple. I think the Michelob compensated for my notoriously poor shooting eye, plus these guys started much earlier than I.

John and his friend, Lou, told me to "bag college and this hiking crap" in favor of life working on the pipeline. They said they were making good money and they got to live their lives without any worries. As they chased their beers with shots of whiskey, lives without boundaries, goals, or direction began to appeal to me. I no longer defended my quest or my aim to finish the Trail. By 11:00, I was too unsteady to find the Trail, even if I knew which way to turn; John invited me to bunk in his trailer which he kept in a nearby campground, "just off your trail," he said.

The three of us closed the tavern at 1:00 AM. In the parking lot, John and Lou traded blows over who was the bigger derelict, but that ended with a group hug, as each of us professed our undying friendship and loyalty.

Lou drove off first, screeching toward the west in a cloud of dust and gravel. We turned east, back towards Frederick, where I started the night. John was driving in the far-left lane.

"Ha, Ha; that's great." I said, "Now what do you say we try the right lane?"

He began swerving back and forth across the four-lane mountain highway; I sobered in a hurry. Ahead the road curved to the left; he made no sign of turning.

"There's a turn up ahead. See the turn? See it?"

He stared blankly at the road, his eyes showing no sign of life. We sped toward the curve. Still he stared ahead. We were going to die. I shot my hand out, grabbed the wheel, and turned it hard to the left. We slid on the shoulder, but found the road.

"I'm okay. I'm okay."

"Hey look, I appreciate all you've done for me - really - but you can let me off anywhere."

The road again turned to the left; in front of us loomed only the guard rail – and the stars beyond. Suddenly, aimlessness was no longer a calling for me; I still can come up with goals worth living for. We closed in, hurtling toward the edge of the cliff. I looked at him, waiting for him to react. His glazed eyes stared at the road. Again, I grabbed the wheel and spun us back on the road.

"Maybe you're right. I'm not okay." He seemed to concentrate better for a few moments, then he looked over at me, "Say, who is this guy sitting next to me? What's he doing here?"

I reached for my pack in the backseat, ready to bail as soon as he slowed down. He braked a little and shifted onto the gravel shoulder, but instead of stopping, he abruptly turned down a steep, twisting dirt road, which I would not have attempted sober in broad daylight.

"Where. Are. You. Going?" I asked, an octave too high, my heart pounding in my chest. The road led to a campground, his campground, but he forgot where he parked his trailer, so he circled the camp twice, once sideswiping a picnic table, before pulling into his site.

I was totally awake at this point. How I missed the simple life in Maine, where one could hike for days without encountering nut jobs like this. He opened the trailer and showed me the spare bunk. Then he pulled out some milk, peanut butter, and crackers.

"Sorry, there's not much else," he said. "I hate to be such a poor host."

"That's the last thing I would accuse you of being."

At seven, I awoke, packed my bag, and was all set to leave when his alarm clock rang: another day on the pipeline.

"Hell with it. I'm not going in. Take it easy, Mountain Man."

A short side trail brought me to the AT, my home and companion. "A foolish consistency" as Emerson said, might be the "hobgoblin of little minds," but not every exit will take me where I need to go. My stomach felt a bit queasy, but I was thankful to be back on the Trail.

SEPTEMBER 2.

The Towering Inferno

Whenever I lose the Trail, the emotion I feel is not fear. Not knowing where I am cannot hurt me, but I feel something in my stomach; I notice a difference in my breathing; and I lose track of time. The shortness of breath I can handle as I search for the right direction, but the slowing down of the world around me adds to the sense of unease. Getting genuinely lost is not easy, considering I am following white blazes painted on trees every hundred feet or so – essentially, I am walking in a series of straight lines. Nevertheless, I have misplaced the Trail more than a few times, although I usually find it before too long. But "lost" opposed to "misplacing the Trail" is something else again. In fact, a person can feel lost while knowing exactly where he stands.

My plan was to reach Harpers Ferry by nightfall, hiking

the seventeen miles from the Washington Monument in the mountains of western Maryland, where I stopped to eat my breakfast of PBJLB, just a few miles after escaping my brief career as a pipeline worker. The past few days have been end of August hot and sticky. I feel miserable and smell worse. To top it off, the Gerry tube with my strawberry jelly swelled with gas. My first thought was botulism, but the bubbles smelled strangely familiar. I risked instantaneous death by tasting it. What do you know? The August heat fermented my jelly. I ate my peanut butter on Logan bread with strawberry wine jelly, a "taste sensation that's sweeping the nation."

I do not know if it was the heat or just my mood, but I was slow to leave the picnic area at the Washington Monument State Park. I chatted with the ranger who walked over to ask if I heard about the fire on Mt. Katahdin. After all the rain and mud I walked through in Maine, I could not imagine a fever burning there. Nevertheless, the park was ablaze. The rangers at Baxter State Park warned us about fire before I spent the month drenched by rain and melting ice. Yet, they knew the winter snows and the spring rains fell short of norms, so the amount of water that soaked into the ground would not last through the dry season.

I described the awesome display of blowdowns in Maine that left trees leaning against one another like rows of dominos. Because years ago, the lumber companies clear cut the forests, the trees that came back grew so close together, that when one died, it fell against the next one, knocking it into another and then another, knocking down trees like rows of dominos. Not all these trees fell to the ground; Maine is filled with thousands of dead trees turned grey, propped against each other. Normally, dead trees fall to the ground and rot, but these trees were left suspended in the air to become seasoned firewood. So long as heavy snows and spring rains fell, the trees were too moist to burn, but the rains that fell on me during June, left the state when I did.

I could have spent the whole day talking about the fire in Maine, or about any other subject for that matter, but it did not make me feel better. I felt remorse, as if caught in a terrible lie. For this past week, I looked for meaning, but found none, no reason to keep hiking other than my worry about what other people might think of me. I found it easier to look for reasons not to hike. The weather, hot and humid, caused me to chafe in all sorts of unpleasant places; and my passion for hiking long since waned.

I have spent time with crazy pipeline workers, with idealistic young people, with kindhearted retirees, and many others from all different places and backgrounds. They shared kindness, generosity, and an appreciation for adventure, although tempered with enough sense to let others trod the treks. They saw me as a heroic figure: the trailblazer, the pioneer, but I see myself as a pathetic Don Quixote, engaged in a quest that means nothing to anyone, a figure too tragic to be comical anymore.

When I flew to Maine, my intention was to hike every step of the Trail, but that pledge ended with the shortcut into Gorham. Then I hiked to find myself, to figure out what I should do for the rest of my life. One thousand miles later, my exact future remains a mystery, but I understand why. All I have done these months is hike. I am well trained to hike for a career, but not to do anything else. Perhaps I could work at a trail shop, but I doubt I would be very good, since I would tell shoppers "These shoes over here will rip your ankles raw, and you see that pack over there, the blue one, that baby will rub the skin right off your back." That is the sum of what I have learned over these past few months.

If I want to fix faucets for a living, I need to get a pipe wrench and start crawling under sinks. If I want to be a lawyer, I need to get into law school – although first I should work for a law firm one summer to see if it is something I would really wish to pursue. The point is, hiking will not tell me what to do or how to do it. I need to get myself to where I can experience the actual work; that is where my real learning will begin. Only by doing or observing will I appreciate whether something is worth doing, at least worth doing by me. I will never know by sitting cross-legged on top of a mountain, contemplating the stars. Up until now, I have been sitting in a lean-to of my own making, creating my own gap between what I have and what I want. It does not much matter whether I walk through the gorge or around it, so long as I am moving toward something. Odd that the very Trail that taught me these truths now keeps me from applying them.

The ranger sensed my anxiety and offered to drive me to Harpers Ferry. I turned him down. The hike promised to be as gentle a seventeen miles as ever I will find. As much as I did not want to spend any more of my life hiking, what is the point of being on a hike if I do not actually hike? But as I walked with him to his car, the temptation proved too strong. I was tired and still hurting from the night's revelry at the tavern. The motivation I found at seven left me by nine. Again, my desperation won: I took the ride.

Upon reaching Harpers Ferry, I visited the Appalachian Trail Headquarters, a small building with a few books for sale. The woman behind the counter saw too many long-distance hikers to become excited about one more, or maybe she could sense that I was no longer a devotee, but again I felt the need to connect with people.

"Hey, have you heard about Steve Jackson?" I asked.

"Why? Did you meet him?"

"Meet him? Why, I owe him my life." With that, she called the others from the back and soon five people surrounded me, all eager to hear about the famous record setter who passed through Harpers Ferry one night, long after quitting time. Steve, who took to leaving his card, rather than waste his precious time signing Trail registers, would never have waited just for the world headquarters of the Appalachian Trail to open the next day.

So, while I was no celebrity in their eyes, I could offer my father's old line: "You can shake the hand of the man, who shook the hand – of Steve Jackson." (Or, at least, who accepted four Pepto Bismal tablets from him.)

I treated them to the story of this intense man who hoped to set the record for quickest time from Maine to Georgia, without the help of anyone else. He carried a small bag with him, so the Pepto Bismal tablets he gave me represented a sizable portion of his gear. Without carrying a heavy pack, he was averaging over forty miles a day, which meant that he did not need to bear the extra weight of food for the long stretches between stores or diners. The longest stretch of unbroken wilderness on the Trail, in Maine, extended over one hundred miles. It took us a week to get through; it took Steve Jackson three days.

After telling my story, I wandered around the tourist area, feeling uncomfortably out of place. I looked and, I am sure, smelled like a Black Lagoon creature, devouring any hapless junk food that foolishly crossed its path.

Everyone moved faster and I could not make out what

anybody was saying. My thoughts slowed; my body felt heavy; and the world blurred past me. Eventually, I gave up trying to seem normal and walked down to the river to read. Families with children visited Harpers Ferry; young lovers strolled down its paths; and I sat on the river bank, too strange to fit in.

Night fell and the streets became deserted. I looked into the store windows seeing only my tired reflection. I called home, telling my parents how my thoughts pivoted from confusion to determination to desperation. I already walked past the point where the Trail helped me; now, only my impatience grew. My father listened to me, then made it clear the decision to continue to hike was up to me. I needed neither his permission nor his approval. I did not even have to tell him.

"You and you alone enjoy the rewards or suffer the pains. Only you will say, 'I hiked the Trail.' So don't waste another moment thinking you have to do this to please anyone else, especially not me."

I guess I placed the responsibility of what to do with my life on others, as if my leaving the Trail would let them down. I spent more energy thinking about how others might feel than how I feel. My pack is heavy enough, without carrying that extra burden. Consumed by the boredom and fatigue of the Trail, and the very real desire to get on with my life, I have no way to understand how I might feel in a week or twenty years from now. I do not want to hold on to this quest, but I am afraid to let it go.

I fell asleep on the banks of the Potomac. Ahead lay forty more miles of roads until I reach Chester Gap, where the smooth trails of the Shenandoah National Park begin. Fall will soon be on its way with its invigorating air and blue skies.

And I will still be hiking.

SEPTEMBER 3.

This Place is for the Byrds

When I awoke at first light in Harper's Ferry yesterday, I was still eighty-two miles north of Rockfish Gap, where I-64 crosses the Blue Ridge Mountains, and from where I plan to hitch into Charlottesville, home to the University of Virginia – my UVA.

But instead of walking, I caught a ride to Linden, Virginia. From there, I hiked about four miles to the Mosby Shelter, where I spent the night. Hiking twenty-five miles today, I reached the Byrd Shelter. In between, I passed the ranger's kiosk at the entrance of the Shenandoah National Park and registered my whereabouts, as the Northbounders warned me to do. I longed for the freedom of Maine, where I could come and go as I pleased. The Shenandoah National Park has too many rules – and so many people.

So, here is a comparison. I broke the rules by hitching to Mosby Shelter, named after John Mosby, who commanded the Confederate First Cavalry, otherwise known as Mosby's Raiders. They broke the rules of engagement, terrorizing the Union army. Of course, Mosby did not see it that way. He saw himself as a cavalier, slicing through the rear guard of the Northern army, disrupting supply and communications, while striking fear into the hearts of the enemy. In the view of his opponents, he broke the fair and honorable rules of war. He did what he needed to win, but then again, his side lost. So, what was his punishment for war crimes and treason? After the war, which he survived, he served the Grant Administration as the US ambassador to Hong Kong, a city I would love to visit after reading *Tai-Pan* and *Noble House* by James Clavell.

I broke the rules of Thruhiking, at least as I see them. If I make it all the way to Springer Mountain, 2100 miles south of Kathadin, I will need to put an asterisk by my record, like Roger Maris, and report that I hiked only 2,000 of them, having skipped nearly 100 more miles over these past few days. That was four to six days of hiking I will never walk. To then say: "I hiked the Appalachian Trail," would be dishonorable. It should at least cost me my ambassadorship to Hong Kong (although I could go for some Chinese food about now.)

I have mixed feelings about my journey through this part of the south. On the grounds of The University of Virginia, under the shadow of Monticello, we think of Virginia as the most important colony in the fight for Independence from Great Britain, not about its critical role in the bitter War Between the States.

I am still many miles away, but I am also about a century removed from Charlottesville. The historical markers and names of roads and shelters, between Gettysburg and Mosby Shelter, keep that fractious period of our nation's history constantly in mind.

President Lincoln went to great lengths to make sure the hostility ended once the war was over. At Appomattox Court House, Grant, Lee, and the other generals shook hands and ended the war; the rebel soldiers were given leave to return to their homes. Those men who ended the war, men of vision, knew that healing and rebuilding the nation was more important than humiliating the already defeated soldiers, a lesson lost on the allies when they dealt with Germany in the 1920s.

I love so many things about the South. What other state is as steeped with honor and tradition as Virginia? And yet, such honorable and learned men, like Washington, Jefferson, Madison, Monroe and Patrick Henry, all who professed a hatred of slavery, still rationalized it as a justifiable means to an end. This brutal business poisoned their society, yet the great men of Virginia gave legal slavery another century of life, even while weaving into the Constitution the means to end it.

Around here, the war is not a forgotten disgraceful episode, but a cherished memory, the gallant war, the war fought to ensure the powers left to the states by the nation's founders. This viewpoint drives me crazy. Whitewashing the real reason we fought the war led to the hundred years of Jim Crow, the Ku Klux Klan, racial inequality, and the perpetuation of a Black underclass ideology that has harmed both people of color and the rest of our country.

The war was fought to perpetuate slavery. Say it.

Admission is the first step to recovery.

SEPTEMBER 8.

Return to Paradise

What possessed a college student – a Wahoo – like me to wake up at dawn, smear Vaseline on my body, and walk all day every day, rather than tuck myself into bed after a night of college fun?

I was lucky that two mornings ago, no ranger caught me sleeping within view of the Byrd shelter; she could have given me a ticket. The shelters were built for Thru-hikers, but because Shenandoah National Park attracts so many visitors – and so many who want to sleep for free in the shelters – the park rangers made all the stone shelters and the area around them off-limits to everyone, Thru-hikers included.

As I packed my bag in the awakening light, I saw I was not the only scofflaw. Strewn about the Byrd Shelter No. 4

meadow, were orange, blue, and red sleeping bags and pup tents of an even wider spectrum of color. All the colors not normally found in nature filled that dew-covered meadow. After yesterday's long hike, I awoke dirty and smelly. Usually, a person cannot smell their own stench, but days without showering, the heat and humidity, wearing the same clothes, and the constant movement made a putrid combination that should attract flies – well, in fact, it does. As I looked at the damp grass, I imagined rolling nude in the morning dew. The weather has been hot and muggy and, despite my Vaseline and baby powder, my back and butt are chafed with strawberries, spots where the pack rubbed my skin raw.

But I skipped the dew bath because I was a man on a mission. I jumped right into a good walking pace, humming school songs, like "Hey Baby" and "It's the same, old song," as I hustled the four miles to Thornton Gap, where I ate breakfast in the lodge.

When I put my pack back on, it dug into the sores that covered my back. So I asked the ranger (or rangerette, as was the case) if she would permit me to leave my pack at the station, hike to Big Meadows, and come back later for it. I told her I needed to hurry to Big Meadows to make a phone call, which was true: my sister was leaving the country the next day, plus, what I did not tell her, I entertained the notion that if I could get there early enough, I could invite some college friends to meet me at Big Meadows for dinner, then drive me back to pick up my pack. Oh, how I wanted to get to UVA, but that would take several more days to hike the seventy-eight miles to Rockfish Gap to get within hitching distance.

The ranger said no; besides, she said, I could call from the next campground, Skyland, ten miles south, where the road to

Luray Caverns crossed the Skyline Drive. Forcing me to play the sympathy card, I pulled up my shirt and showed her my back.

"All right," she said in disgust, "leave your pack."

I walk much faster without the pack – in fact, I can almost fly – and without the pack, there was no rubbing with each step, giving my strawberries the chance to heal. Moreover, as there was less weight on my feet, my blisters could heal as well. All summer long I trained for a day like this, soaring past everyone as effortlessly as a hawk circling in the sky. Someday, I promised myself, I would hike a long distance carrying only a small bag: no sleeping bag, just a space blanket; no pots or stove; and no more than two days' food at a time – and maybe some Pepto-Bismol tablets. I also will never walk in heavy boots again. There was no need, especially over the smooth park trails of the Shenandoah. All I need is a basketball shoe upper on a Vibram sole, with plenty of arch support and enough ankle support to keep my foot from rolling over. Plus, it must be able to dry fast, as it will get wet on the Appalachian Trail.

Hiking through the Shenandoah is a vacation from the rigors of the rest of the Trail, notwithstanding the crowds of people who head here for the summer. We owe a deep gratitude to past generations for kicking off the rightful owners and preserving these tracts of land. When it comes to land use decisions, maybe the final arbiter is time.

When I passed the Skyland campground, where Route 211 crosses Skyline Drive, I thought about hitching west into Luray where I visited the Luray Caverns ten years ago. The guided tour takes the visitor into the center of the mountain, through a cavern filled with formations of stalactites and stalagmites, although do not ask me which is up and which is down, and, if I recall correctly, there was a car museum underground as well.

I remember it was blistering hot as we crossed the parking lot, but when we descended into the Cavern, the temperature dropped so much that my mom wore a sweatshirt down there. I also remember a rock formation called "Fried Eggs," which looked like fried eggs.

The problem with frying eggs on the Trail is that the eggs stick to the aluminum pans, forcing us to waste time scrubbing. So, when I want to cook an egg, I use some of my Boy Scout tricks. The idea is to cook the eggs in edible pots, directly on the coals. The best tasting is to take a large onion, cut it in half and remove all but the peel and the outer two layers. Make a fire and form a doughnut hole amidst the coals. Place the hollowed onion in the doughnut hole. It works best by having some larger logs on either side of the coals to contain and radiate the heat. Finally, crack an egg into the cavity of the onion. The egg will finish cooking long before the outer layers burn. Discard the outermost charred onion skin and enjoy the inner onion and the flavored egg. This also works with an orange skin.

I have also hard boiled an egg in a paper cup filled with water. The boiling water keeps the cup from burning, although as the water evaporates, the paper burns, but stays intact long enough to cook the egg.

As I approached Big Meadows, I met Ashby Phillips and his son, Boog, who were walking north along the Trail. I guess with my beard and bulging leg muscles, I looked to them like "Mountain Man" once again. Mr. Phillips stopped me to ask if he could ask me some questions. He then asked if they could walk with me to Big Meadows, so I slowed my pace to allow him to continue to pepper me with questions, as if I were part of an educational exhibit. Every time I would say something, Phillips would turn to his son and say, "Did you hear that, Boog?"

"So, what state did you find the most difficult?"

"That would be Pennsylvania, because of the long stretches without water and because the rocks ground down the soles of my boots."

"Did you hear that, Boog? The rocks ground down his shoes."

"How did you get food along the way?"

"I mailed myself boxes of food to post offices near the Trail."

"Did you hear that, Boog? He mailed himself boxes."

Of course, he heard it, he's standing right next to us, but I said that in my thoughts – not out loud – for once.

I left them at the edge of the Big Meadows campground and continued to the washhouse where I washed my face with cold water. There I chatted with a retired New Englander, Mr. Palmer, who reminisced about his own hikes through the White Mountains. He offered me a space by his trailer, if I made it back with my pack.

Using the pay phone in the visitor center, I got the chance to speak with my sister Rebecca, who takes off in a few days for her own great adventure to work on a kibbutz in Israel. I enjoyed a great time with her and the rest of my family when I left the Trail at Hawk Mountain, but I still wanted one last chance to say goodbye.

Hitchhiking is another one of those activities not permitted in the park, so retrieving my pack would not be easy. I approached people in the parking lot, which was a little aggressive, but I started it off by saying, "Hi, I'm a Thru-hiker, hiking the Appalachian Trail and I left something behind at the ranger station at Thornton Gap. Are you driving north?"

Despite the awkwardness, I made the thirty-six-mile round trip with time to spare before dark. Back at Big Meadows, I took a hot shower, then went to the lodge where I drank a Moonshine Zombie and made my other call.

When at college, I live in a big white house with a huge lawn called The Anchorage, located not far from the football stadium. The twelve to fifteen of us – it varies – have an unofficial fraternity: no rushing, no hazing, just lots of parties and we play volleyball after dinner. It was there that I packaged the food I would later ship to the post offices along the Trail.

Calling by the cheapest method, station-to-station, the operator asked, "Anyone accept a call?"

Anxious to the point of tears, I waited while the person on the other end hemmed and hawed about whether he would accept the call. Wow, some friend. Finally, I yelled to the operator, "Tell him I'll pay for the damn call when I get there."

With that assurance, Rand, my old hiking partner, accepted the call. He must have slipped past me when I left the Trail a few weeks back. He gave the phone to one of the other guys.

The scene reminded me of the time Jack Benny was held up at gun point. The robber demanded, "Your money or your life."

Benny, a noted miser, did not reply.

The robber poked him with his gun and asked, "Well?"

Jack Benny replied, "I'm thinking! I'm thinking!"

No one thought my idea to drive to Big Meadows for dinner was all that great. "After all, Dave, it is a school night, and the round trip would be over eighty miles."

Getting together with my UVA friends will just have to wait a few more days until I reach Route 250 at Rockfish Gap.

Solitude is one thing, but I was no longer alone in the Maine wilderness. Although I passed someone roughly every forty-five seconds, I felt lonelier than I did in the 100-mile wilderness in Maine. There were so many people in the Shenandoah that seeing another human was no longer a novelty. During the first part of the trip, seeing another person was a happening worthy of celebration; here, not so much.

Part of the problem was that as a hardened Thru-hiker, I walk too fast for any weekender to keep up, so walking with someone was out of the question. I needed to keep the pace fast so I could reach Rockfish Gap.

On the other hand, back when I was isolated, I could sink into my thoughts; here in the Shenandoah, too many people break my trance asking me a question, saying hello, or giving me their support. I feel like a postal worker. If I could perform my repetitive task without disruption, I might survive. In reality -- my reality -- there was nothing about the Trail I cared to be aware of anymore and I did not need these people bringing me back to the moment.

It is not people, I miss. What I miss, is a *second conversation*, one that breaks through the barrier of conventional chitchat, the "Hi. How's the weather" discussion. That is not real communication. But to go further with a person, I need to develop some level of trust. Without that trust, conversation can be an assault. I can't stop somebody along the Trail and start saying, "Hi. How are you? I'm a Taurus. I'm from Philadelphia: I like baseball, cheesesteaks – I went to Central High. How about you? Boy, I sure miss spending time with girls. I like girls. How about you? No? That's okay. No big deal, really." If I were to do that, a Park Ranger would shoot me with a tranquilizer dart.

No, a *second conversation* needs to be coaxed onto the line. Once there, it can unleash the thoughts and emotions that lay suppressed within my soul. There are few things in life I treasure more than a good conversation, for between those talks, I spend a lot of time with myself. I awake with the sun, hike twenty or thirty miles, then fall asleep by dusk. That does not leave much time for talking.

Outside of my family members, and that young woman in Dartmouth with her unused waterbed, I have not talked deeply with anyone in three months. I guess I could include Steve and Al, a few of the camp counselors at Eagle Spring, Father Blue at Graymoor – and the conversation around the Mystery woman's dinner table. But that is it. Have I learned what anyone else fears or loves or what anyone hopes to be doing in three years? How do people think, do they discuss logically or with emotion? What are their prejudices? How does their sense of humor work? Do they create routines or are they repulsed by them?

In fact, I do not know much about anyone. When I meet someone, I share some personal biography and recent history – mostly of the geographic variety. But all that should be a prelude to the *second conversation*, but I never get to hang around long enough to have one. Being friendly is not the same as being friends.

I miss the warm moments of friendship that I thought I would experience along the Trail, like staring into the dying embers of a campfire or trying to find the patterns in stars. I want someone to share a scenic overlook with me. I want someone to care about, and someone to care about me. Sitting alone, drinking that Moonshine Zombie at Big Meadows, I longed to be back at school laughing with friends. I suppose, of everything I miss, I miss laughter the most. Hiking alone has become very solemn.

When I get back to school, I will look up a resident advisor in my old dorm. She stored her stuff in my room over the summer and I would like to be the one to help her move it back. What a bright, sweet, and lovely young woman; we have been friends up to now, but who knows where that could go? What a fool am I for casting myself out into the wilderness, when the true adventure lies so much closer to home.

After finishing my second Moonshine Zombie, I walked to the Palmer's campsite. As I approached, I overheard people talking about me as if I were some returning hero. It turned out that the Palmer's trailer was parked right next to the Phillips's – little Boog's family. With the thousands of people camping in the National Park, the two families I met earlier happen to be sharing a campfire that night. You can't make this stuff up.

I entered the light of the fire and they all stood up to greet me. After that, I regaled them with tales of the Trail, like the time I came face to face with that teenage moose in Maine. (Did you hear that, Boog? He came face to face with a moose – in Maine!) When we all said our good nights, I laid my ground cloth and unrolled my sleeping bag on the grass and went to sleep, content to be among friends.

The next morning, while eating a big country breakfast made by Mrs. Phillips, Mr. Palmer asked me, "Where would you like your pack left today?" They were heading south so I suggested the ranger station at Swift Run Gap, at Route 33, nineteen miles south and almost a third of the way to Rockfish Gap and UVA. Without a pack, I figured I could reach the Gap in about six hours, even with a stop here and there. After that I could hike with the pack until the daylight faded. By that time, I should reach the shelter at High Top Mountain. Anyway, that is what I figured.

Boog and his dad hiked with me to the outskirts of Big Meadows, then we shook hands and they turned back. My family once camped at Big Meadows when I was around Boog's age. I remembered the Appalachian Trail went right past our campsite. As I walked, I tried to remember where we camped, but the years changed the park and it was much more crowded. That is the problem with success. The national parks, as Yogi Berra might have said, are "so crowded, nobody wants to go there anymore."

I remember when my infant brother got fed up with us and decided to go home on his own. Fortunately for my frantic mother, some people walking on the Appalachian Trail told her they saw a baby crawling north about one hundred yards up the Trail; the little coot was making a break for it. After that incident, my mother devised a harness for him and kept him tethered to a birch tree. He filled his time by sucking on the stub of a pine branch. That was the same pine tree, although a different stub, on which we looped the handle of the three-gallon Coleman thermos.

We were camped at the bottom of a steep slope, a long way to the wash house, especially carrying the three-gallon thermos and the five-gallon white plastic water container. I thought about that hill constantly. At about eight pounds a gallon, that five-gallon jug weighed over forty pounds and it was so big, I could barely lift it off the ground. It was a long walk up the hill and then an even longer one down, carrying the filled containers.

To make matters worse, we attended an evening campfire, at which the Ranger told us about the Park's bears:

- Never feed the bears! You will not have enough food to satisfy them and one might show its dissatisfaction by taking a swat at you or maybe chomp your arm. (We have a big black and white cat who operates like that.)
- Never step between a mother bear and her cubs, because she will maul first and ask questions later.
- Never try to escape a bear by climbing a tree, as they can climb faster than you.
- And do not even think about outrunning a bear uphill. Their hind legs are much larger than their front, so they can run uphill much faster than you can.

Your only chance of outrunning a bear is to run down-hill, because they may tumble, head-over-heels, because of their larger hind legs. So, the big question running through my mind, was, "How was I supposed to run downhill, when our campsite was already at the bottom of the hill?" I figured I would have to run uphill, then just before the bear caught me, turn around and run downhill, repeating this until the bear finally fell head-over-heels, knocking itself out.)

After my brother's failed escape, it seemed my sister and I filled those water jugs a lot more often each day. It did not make sense. There were six of us of whom four were kids. If my parents together weighed 400 pounds and the four of us kids averaged 100 pounds (remember one of us was two-and-a-half years of trouble) at a minimum we were going through 2.5 ounces for every pound of person per day. That is more than twice the recommended consumption and about ten times what I would carry with me through parts of Pennsylvania and New York – not that I recommend it. We did not shower with this water, we just used it to drink, make meals, and clean dishes. Up that long hill and then down, with my big sister and I alternating who carried the five-gallon jug.

We slept in two tents; my big sister Beth and I in the pup tent, while the rest of the family slept in the big blue family tent. After listening to the bear talk, my father brought the legendary Mark One into his tent that night. The Mark One was his Navy-issued knife, the size and shape of a Bowie Knife with a sharp cutting edge.

When I saw him bringing the knife into the tent, I said, "Dad. It's 1967; aren't we a bit late to be playing Davey Crocket?"

"I'm not going to "kill me a b'ar," if a bear comes in the front, I'm cutting a door through the back to get the hell out."

We never did have a bear wander into our campsite, but we did have ourselves a genuine, live animal confrontation. My sister and I were in our sleeping bags when a shadow passed a few feet away.

I said, "I think a cat just walked by."

"I don't think that was a cat," she said.

My parents, sitting at the picnic table, stopped talking and probably stopped breathing as a skunk waddled toward them. But their anxiety rose to a yet higher pitch when they heard a noise coming from the direction of the trash can. Emerging into the light of the lantern, sauntered a raccoon, either well satisfied from the garbage or maybe frustrated from the sealed cans -- my parent never asked -- as the only thoughts going through their brains were of baths in tomato juice.

Innocents are caught in the middle of conflicts all the time. Villages are bombed because of faulty coordinates. Bullies pick on the meek. Once when I was in kindergarten, I walked into my classroom that was particularly noisy. Not seeing the teacher, a woman we affectionately called, "Mean Miss Green," who by then was at least a hundred years old, I took it upon myself, as a five-year-old, to yell, "Everybody – keep – quiet!"

Miss Green, who stood not much taller than a five-year-old, emerged from behind an easel and grabbed hold of my ear lobe, hissing, "You're making more noise than the rest of them." So, I know all about innocents getting caught in the crossfire.

My sister and I could see the emerging battle from the pup tent. The lantern cast a circular glow that encompassed the area around the picnic table, creating an illuminated ring into which stepped the two combatants. No one dared utter a sound. The skunk moved its head from left to right as if feigning a maneuver. The raccoon just stopped and stared; its hind quarters rising over its fore.

From where the skunk was positioned, if it fired a stink missile directly at the raccoon, my parents would avoid a direct hit. But that is not how a skunk operates. It must spin around to face away from its quarry, raise its fluffy tail, and then squeeze the sack of stink juice that it carries at the base of its tail. Facing away from the target, precludes pinpoint accuracy, so the skunk has evolved to spray in an angular cone that would spread to include, not only its intended target, but the picnic table as well. I have learned that a skunk can reach a target at ten feet. If the spray leaves the anal gland at a sixty-degree angle that would mean, at ten feet, someone sitting six feet on either side of the raccoon would receive the same amount of spray as the raccoon, assuming no wind. At least one of my parents was within that range. Poor Mom.

The skunk did not turn around; instead it feigned indifference, scanning the ground for bits of human delicacies. Finding none, it seemed to shrug, and walked back in the direction it came. The raccoon looked at my parents, and a moment of relief passed between them, then he too turned and walked in the direction from whence he came.

Before the establishment of the National Park system, the Shenandoah was a mountaintop community of farms with orchards and grazing lands. I picked some apples from an orchard abandoned decades before. To this day, descendants of those pioneers bury their dead in a small cemetery I passed on top of the ridge. I wonder how it was they left their farms, by force or by choice? Did the government give them enough money so they could retire to Florida, or were they shifted from self-sufficient farmers to low skilled laborers? I thought about the Delaware Water Gap and wondered if a new national park, as wonderful and beautiful thought they are, was worth the pain inflicted on the few who lived there first.

I passed a side trail called the Bear Rock Scramble. My dad and I hiked this when I was a kid. It must have frightened my father to see his kids silhouetted by nothingness. Just as each of us must gradually get used to heights, so do parents. As I walked through the Shenandoah, I found that compared to the cliffs I climbed in Maine, the Bear Rock Scramble was now just a cub.

My dad smoked a pipe in those days and on the Scramble, we shared the one thin army surplus canteen, which I carried on a thin cord strung around my neck. At one point into the hike on that hot summer day – again, I was Boog's age – I emptied the remaining water onto the ground.

"What the hell are you doing?"

"It tastes terrible, Dad. It tastes like tobacco."

"It tasted fine to me!" My dad bought me my own canteen after that.

Back to Big Meadows – we finally figured out why we were going through water so quickly. After his failed escape, my mom did not bind my brother like his Biblical namesake, Isaac, but rather tethered him to a tree with a fifteen-foot cord tied in a loop, so he could move in a 360 degree circle (as if there were any other type). That gave him over seven hundred square feet to explore, but that was not nearly enough for his crafty, almost three-year old criminal mind. Whenever he thought no one was paying attention, this Moriarty would waddle to the pine tree where we hung the thermos and enjoy his new game of "Press the Button," so that big brother and sister would have to climb the mountain again. When we caught him in the act, my mother shortened the little Napoleon's leash, so he was left master of a realm reduced to 531 square feet. He was none too happy.

I ate lunch at the Lewis Mountain Campground, which I learned was built for what were called at that time "Coloreds" – separate and not so equal. Hard to imagine what a legacy like that does to people – I have not passed a single Black person hiking the Trail from Maine down to here.

We would have been better off, as a country, if slavery never existed, but it did exist, and so the challenge has been to create a democracy that will judge a person by the content of his character and not by the color of his skin. We tell the people of the world to be free, to be like us, but we have left so much of our history tarnished with slavery, Indian wars, and racial and religious intolerance, that our past needs a lot of polishing before we can put it on display. The rest of the world won't listen if we declare, "Do as we say not as we do."

There is a difference between the sins of "omission" and the sins of "commission." The person who steals or cheats commits the crime – that is "commission." But the person, who after witnessing the crime, remains silent, is also guilty. That person has committed the sin of "omission," he fails to act. When we stopped importing slaves and finally ended slavery, at that point we no longer were guilty of the sins of commission. But for the next hundred years, we tolerated a part of our society to live outside or, rather, beneath the rest of our society; for that, we were guilty of the sin of "omission." "You are either part of the solution or you are part of the problem," as my father would say.

When I was within three miles of Swift Run Gap, where my pack awaited me at the ranger station, I began to hear the low rumble of an approaching storm. Dark thunder clouds boiled overhead. The wind picked up strength and lightening crackled above the tree tops. I knew I should not stand under a tree, but standing in a clearing on top of a mountain would be even more dangerous. I ran. The Trail became a small river as I sloshed along the last few miles. I could barely see through the driving rain, but I kept going because I knew dry clothes awaited me. By the time I reached the station, the storm passed. I gave the ranger a big sopping grin and asked for my pack. He pointed to it, leaning against a post one hundred feet away, in the open – exposed – my pack.

Everything got wet. I spent the next six hours squeezing the water from my socks, drinking hot tea, and talking to Tom Rutledge, the night shift ranger. (I didn't say another word to the day shift idiot who watched my pack sit in the rain.)

I cooked dinner and shared some with Tom. He explained the different classifications of rangers, how some were naturalists and others were law enforcement. He was of the latter variety. When I was ten, the Shenandoah rangers took us on nature hikes and told us about bears at their campfire talks. Tom said that type of ranger was a vanishing species. Now the park rangers stop poachers who shoot the deer and steal the ginseng that grows wild in the park. He also said the parks have become havens for thieves, drug dealers, and motorcycle gangs. That is how democratic our park system has become, everyone can enjoy it.

At about 10:30 PM, I said goodbye, partly happy over an evening of good company, partly annoyed that I wasted six hours I could have spent hiking toward Rockfish Gap, the closest point to Charlottesville. With six hours more walking, I could have been at least twelve miles closer to UVA.

Tom suggested, "Why don't you hitch to Charlottesville from here. That way you don't have to hike tomorrow in wet clothes?" Route 33, which goes past the station, reaches Route 29, which goes south through UVA.

I was not so sure I wanted a ride from anyone who would pick me up that late at night, but the area was well lit and after fifteen minutes of trying, a traveling salesman stopped for me. Forty minutes later I was walking by Memorial Gym up Emmet Street, right in the heart of The University. After three months of falling asleep at dusk and awakening at dawn, I forgot how my life used to be. At 11:30 at night, people were playing tennis, riding bikes, and enjoying life. This was indeed paradise. And the welcomes I received from my friends made me wonder why I took a semester off from this terrific place and whether I could ever leave it again.

CHAPTER FIVE

Renewal

SEPTEMBER 9.

The University

The first time I came to Charlottesville was by the Southern Crescent, the train that started at Union Station in Washington, DC, and continued on its way to New Orleans. I got off that train onto a dark platform, with no signs and no one around to ask which direction I needed to go. When I got to the street, lugging my suitcase, there were similarly no suggestions as to whether I should turn right or left to find The University. I turned left, figuring that if in five minutes I did not see a sign of a college, I would turn around.

It was April of my senior year of high school. Of the four colleges I applied to, three were Ivies, so they would not send their acceptances until the fifteenth of April. The fourth, UVA, not only accepted me by the end of March, it accepted me into the Echols Scholar program. The Dean of the program, Charles Vandersee, invited me to stay in the dorm with the current batch of first year Echols Scholars. When I took the train to Charlottesville, missing three days of school, I was like most high school seniors who could not understand the point of high school once college acceptances were dealt.

Within five minutes of walking, I could see the glow of lights ahead, but still no signs. Approaching a train trestle and climbing a steep slope, I saw shops on one side of the street and medical buildings on the other. Each shop was filled with students enjoying grilled donuts, deep fried, batter-dipped mushrooms, hamburgers topped with eggs, and the other fine foods I would one day learn to love.

I stopped a young man and woman to ask them to point me toward the Dunnington dorm. They said they could walk me most of the way, since they lived in the "Old Dorms" and Dunnington was a "New Dorm."

They questioned whether I was visiting UVA for Easters Weekend. I felt bad having to correct them, "Easter was last week."

"No, not Easter – Easters," they corrected, and then took turns filling me in on the strange and exciting lore of this enchanted place.

"All Easters Weekend" was known as the "second largest party in the county after the Mardi Gras." It consists of bands, beer, mud, dancing, and whatever else goes on with that combination. I unknowingly stumbled onto a weekend of great fun, if you are a student, and wanton madness, if you are an adult.

The grand finale of Easters takes place in the sunken field behind Madison Hall, known as "Mad Bowl." It was an afternoon of music, dancing, and a giant mud bath, which I could visit only briefly since I was heading to the railroad station to catch the train back home. What an overwhelming sight for a public school kid from Philly. Did it influence my decision? No; I made my choice soon after getting there.

On that very first morning, walking across the Ed School Bridge over Emmet Street, I passed an attractive young woman with lovely yellow hair who smiled at me as she walked by. Now, having grown up in a big city, taking busses in the afternoon gloom, and attending an all-boy public high school, I was not accustomed to having a pretty young woman smile at me.

"Excuse me, Miss," I said, "But do you know me?

"No."

"But you smiled at me?"

"Yes."

"But you don't know me?"

I called home that night and said, "Dad, this is the place."

And it was from that same place that, after the two best years of my life, I left to hike alone in the woods.

SEPTEMBER 10.

The Anchorage

The Anchorage: home to loud music, big dinners, volley-ball – and me. This great white hovel has been my home while I attended the University of Virginia. Actually, somewhere from ten to fourteen of us lived in what was once a fashion-able house on the Virginia Garden Tour and, at other times, an unfashionable house on the UVA frat tour. But its history has been so tarnished, that by the time I moved here, it no longer held even that distinction.

At one time, the famous Admiral Mathew Fontaine Maury, one of the great navigators and racists of our country, lived there. But during the years since, the Anchorage passed from owner to owner until in 1956, a fraternity, the "Zebes," Zeta Beta Tau, moved in. Just as the Greeks devastated their rocky homeland, so they did the Anchorage. They enclosed the once beautiful winding staircase with a plaster fire wall (further marred by a gaping hole where a football player practiced his blocks). This was not too bad, I suppose, because the steps were already ruined by the brothers riding their motorcycles upstairs to their rooms. To afford the purchase, the frater-nity sold the lower gardens to a developer. Where once grew zinnias and roses, now stood parked cars and dumpsters. Still, I loved the old place, although I needed to lay plastic tarps on the flat roof over my room to keep the rain from pouring through. And I wore an extra sweater – or sometimes a down jacket – when I studied in my room during the winter. The two space heaters my roommate George and I bought from Dart Drugs, brought the midwinter temperature up to 37° in what was once an unheated glass enclosed porch. And when a window broke, we covered it with a board; and when the plaster fell from the ceiling, we would sweep away the mess thankful that no one got hurt, and after a while we did not even mind the peanut-butter brown paneling that the fraternity put up years ago, to cover the cracked and crumbling plaster walls.

At the end of my first year, when my Dad drove down to bring me home, we swung by the Anchorage so I could show him my new home. I could see his concerned gaze at the empty whiskey bottles and the scattered beer kegs, the cracked ceilings, and the peeling paint. No eye for character, that man. When my next roommate George asked him how he liked it, my dad replied, "I haven't seen anything like it since – *The Grapes of Wrath*."

According to the stories I heard – and I was not there – the Zebes were known for selling, if not using, every type of drug known to man. This was truly where "students, townspeople and tourists" met. As a consequence, a lot of money flowed through the Anchorage and weekly grain parties became the norm. On occasion, they would fill the sunken living room with sand, plant a few potted palms, and hand everyone a bottle of baby oil.

Rumors flew around town that the Zebes were running a brothel one summer. As probable as it may have seemed, this just was not the case. The Zebes sublet some rooms to a couple of girls from Executive Massage, a legitimate massage parlor in town. Not wanting to lose touch with their work, they would handle a few clients on their days off. Well, everyone knows how people will talk, so the nasty rumors spread. Apparently, they rubbed a few people the wrong way, but I am here to say that the Zebes were not running the brothel, just subleasing space. In 1974 the police raided the Anchorage for the last time. The Dean of Students finally got his wish and closed the fraternity down.

By the time I moved in, the Anchorage operated as a non-fraternity, "an autonomous collective," as my Allentown friend Mark would say, in a high, British voice. The fifteen or ten or whatever number we totaled from time to time, paid four hundred dollars a month rent – total – something that will forever ruin my perspective on real estate prices.

During football season, we would divert traffic onto our ample lawn and charge a buck a car. When the University announced it would close the Mad Bowl party after my first year, because it was attracting too many people from the outside (like me, I suppose), we came up with the idea of holding a party, for five hundred of our closest and dearest friends, right on the lawn of the Anchorage. We sold tee-shirts designed by another friend, the graphic artist, Pete Brehm, for five dollars apiece, which entitled the wearer to music, dancing, and all the beer he or she could drink. Since we were next to the football stadium, we were in easy walking distance of all the dorms on our side of the University. Not only did we save Easters, we did so without creating a crowd problem, and we made some money to boot. Nothing wrong with some honest pay for an honest day's work.

We took turns shopping for food. Each of us cooked for the group once every two to three weeks and, in return, we ate some awesome food. We used some of our parking revenues to butcher a side of beef, sold to us by my enterprising roommate and look-alike, George, which kept us fed at wholesale prices. After dinners, we would play volleyball.

Our games were different than those in the intramural league. We did not follow the International Volleyball

146

Association's rules, nor did we use the AAU rules for that matter. Instead we played by "Anchorage Rules." The Anchorage rulebook, in fact, contained only one rule: "There are no rules." Thus, our games more resembled free-for-alls than volleyball games. We sure jumped, spiked, and dove – but mostly laughed. The net was tattered from years of misuse, but its condition was no worse than the rest of the house, so it belonged.

I belonged there too. The guys were so happy to see me, they did not even bill me for meals. I slept in the living room, because I sublet my side of the bedroom to Steve Oliner. I will take Steve's place next semester when he studies abroad in England, which was my plan all along. All I ever wanted to do was study in England. One setback and I gave up on my dream to go along with someone else's dream. How hard would it have been to say, "Thanks, but no. I will try again to achieve my dream."

Of course, either way, I would miss a semester at UVA and living in the crazy dilapidated Anchorage. Besides the food, parties, and volleyball, our time together at the Anchorage gave rise to serious discussions and debates across a wide range of issues: religion, public policy, science, music, and culture. Across the first floor from me, living in the opposite enclosed porch, the one that did not leak, were my friends Mark Booz from Allentown and Mark Klamer from the great baseball city of St. Louis. They both lived next door to me in Dunnington, our first-year dorm, although on opposite sides.

Both of these young men were self-professed conservatives. I grew up in a city that voted heavily Democratic, and in a household where both parents worked in social services – so we tended to self-identify as liberals. In fact, growing up in

Philadelphia, I do not remember ever meeting a conservative.

Whenever we talked about anything, and we talked about everything, the two Marks took a perspective that was usually different from mine. We differed on our opinions, but never with rancor or condescension.

For example, I remember commenting about the waste in restaurants and department stores, when so many people could not afford a decent meal. Mark Klamer responded that whenever a well-intentioned governmental authority tried to control waste, that is, allocate resources, unintended consequences occurred. He said, suppose you want to reduce the excessive usage of paper by limiting the printing of books. Who should say how many *Bibles* get printed or how many copies of *The Godfather*? Who makes the decision over how many heart doctors to train versus urologists? I never thought to compare urologists to Bibles, but Klamer could find the economic principle at the heart of every discussion. Allocation of resources, I see now, is at the heart of economic class struggle. Do we manually allocate wealth and economic decisions, ordering people to do things and punishing them if they do not, or do we allow the "Invisible Hand" of the market to shape behaviors for us? If we are concerned over the fairness of who gets what, is controlling the production the best way to do this?

The first night I got back, I dropped by my old dorm to visit the young woman who stored her boxes in my room over the summer. The hug she gave me made my head spin; she was genuinely happy to see me.

The next night she stopped over to the Anchorage with a cake she baked as her way of thanking us for storing her things over the summer. There she was, this attractive, dynamic young woman surrounded by six or so young men, all in love with her. I wanted to walk her back to the dorm, so we could spend some time alone. But Mark Klamer took me aside and reasoned that since I was heading back to the Trail and will not be back until January, I would only get my hopes up – "Think of how tormented you will be on top of some mountain." He, on the other hand, was staying put, so it would only make sense, for all involved, for him to walk her back, so he reasoned.

Every so often you make a decision in life you know will torment you forever. Over all God's creations: the waterfalls, the sunsets, the crystal-clear mountain lakes – I would take the love of a beautiful woman over all of them. In retrospect, I should have taken the torment over rational acceptance.

I went to Central High in Philadelphia, an all-boy public high school. I was lucky to meet a terrific girl at a sweet sixteen party, otherwise I might have spent high school alone. She and I spoke on the phone until all hours of the night; she owned her own number and could lay in bed talking, whereas I tied up the one line into our house and sat in the kitchen. She was a grade ahead of me and so left for college before my senior year.

Girl's High is one block away, but it was hardly our sister school. The administrators colluded to keep us separate. There was only one school dance in four years and the schools operated on different schedules, so there was no chance of meeting a girl on the bus. Both schools drew from all over the city, but because we were so separate, there was no chance to meet a girl from a different neighborhood. Although my girlfriend attended a school one block away, I never saw her during the week, because it would have meant waiting an hour on the steps of her school before we each took our buses heading in opposite directions, to our separate neighborhoods.

The real loss from going to an all-boy high school was not

just limiting the dating pool, but it was more about not work-ing alongside girls. We did not see them in class and so did not see them as smart, funny, or accomplished. They were limited to being objects of our teenage desires.

My high school is the second oldest public high school in the country. The students need to qualify to get in – and there were no girls – all boys. Four years of school without the oppo-site gender can create a lot of harmful attitudes in just a few years.

When I got to college, I found an equal number of women to men in my class. The University of Virginia used to be an all-male public college, but four years before I got there, they opened admission to undergraduate women. They took it slow, gradually increasing the number of females each year as they built new facilities to accommodate them, like the "New Dorms" I lived in.

Before my time, the UVA men, especially those in the fraternities, went "Down the Road" to visit one of the many women's colleges that encircled UVA. I went on one of these "Road Trips" when I pledged the Delta Upsilon fraternity. The older brothers piled us into the back of a U-Haul truck, threw in a keg of beer, and drove to a women's college, James Madi-son, up and over the Shenandoah National Park, crossing the Appalachian Trail on the same Route 33 from where I hitched my ride.

It was an awful night. About forty of us and maybe ten women from James Madison crowded into two motel rooms. The music and the talking made it hard to hear and there was no room to dance. You either talked with the woman you were pressed up against or you stared at the muted TV. All I thought about was how I left a dorm with sixty of the most beautiful, intelligent, interesting women I would ever meet to travel three hours in the back of a closed U-Haul truck, so I could not hear a word this young lady, whom I would never see again, was saying.

When I got back – alive – I swore I would never waste another night like that. Road trips were a way of life when there were no women roaming the grounds of UVA. The social life in the old days consisted of driving hours to one of the several women's colleges to see young women paraded in front of you, as if from a police lineup. But you didn't get to say, "Sorry, I don't see the one I'm looking for in the lineup, send in the next group of perps." You needed to make a quick decision, because these were all you would see that night. I, on the other hand, went to class with women, ate at the dining hall with them, and fell in love with them on an average of once every thirteen and a half seconds.

I go to school with amazing female classmates. There is a woman in my class who is at least six feet tall, strikingly beautiful, with blonde hair and blue eyes and calls herself "Tequila." She is probably the most confident person I have ever met.

There is another young woman who visited my dorm first year to see her old boyfriend from high school. She is a comet, shooting across the heavens, leaving everyone else in her dust. I have never met anyone with as much charisma. When she becomes the first female president, or the star of the nightly news, I will tell everybody who will listen, I knew Katie Couric way back when.

My Chinese Political Theory class consisted of six people. One of them was my friend Mark from Allentown. Two of the others were women. Both were incredibly smart and well organized. There was Andrea Knox, sharp, quick witted, and a student leader. The other, named Kimberly, wore stunning dresses, as if she were on her way to a wedding afterwards. When the sunlight hit her hair in a certain way, she radiated, like she was crowned with a halo. And just when her appearance would mesmerize you, she would nail you in a discussion. Beauty, brains, and power; it hardly seemed fair. Yet, I met so many young women like this, just walking around, eating at the dining hall, and sitting in class, it made no sense to follow an archaic mating ritual.

I guess they keep us separate in high schools, like the one I went to, so we do not have to feel inferior by comparison, but in the long run, maybe it would have been better to have been exposed to young women early, so we could learn to appreciate them for all their qualities. Otherwise, the separation makes us hunger for women, like caged tigers hunger for meat.

Societies that hide women from males, not only distort a young man's view of women, they weaken the society, because they start each day at half strength. How many works of art or scientific discoveries will these societies never create, because they encourage men to shove their women into the equivalent of prisons? A man who claims he cannot sit with a woman in class, on a bus, or at work, because doing so would mean he could not concentrate, is a coward. The test of a real man is that he can appreciate both the beauty and the intelligence of women, and still produce at his highest value, and later, join them in love, as they go forth together to make a better world.

America has shown other countries how to involve all its people in society. It took us a while. But at the heart of our belief, is that every person, no matter which bathroom we use, or how we pray, or the color of our skin, has something to offer, and we are made stronger because of this contribution. This is what binds us together.

We live in a competitive world and we need to make sure that we train our best people to invent the next products, write the next hit movies, or design the new look for next year. Meeting so many intelligent women, who are fully engaged with life at UVA, fills me with confidence over our nation's future. Our comparative advantage is not some natural resource like oil, but the dynamism of our people. Tough luck, for those societies that still do not get it.

SEPTEMBER 11.

High atop High Top Mountain

Looking west over the Shenandoah Valley, as the setting sun paints the sky pink and violet, I sit propped against my pack, cooled by the evening breeze. As I write, I look out over hundreds of miles of God's green earth.

I begin this final phase of my journey with the promise of fall weather – cool, crisp, and clear. I will need to bear down from here on; I will have to walk over twenty miles a day, for the next forty days, without a day off, to reach Springer Mountain before winter sets in, all the while keeping the good times from my week at UVA playing in my head.

Those good times were not without interruption. As Mark from Allentown and I walked through Newcomb Hall, the student center, a fellow from my first-year dorm pushed through the crowd of people to reach me.

"Hi Craig," I said.

He shook with rage and spoke with such fury, spittle flew from his mouth. "What are you doing here? You need to get back on the Trail. There's too much temptation here; it's too soft. Don't you get how many of us are living our lives through you?"

"What?" I said. "Listen pal, don't live your life through me: not you or anyone else. What I choose to do or not do is for me alone to decide. You don't get a vote."

Mark pulled me away before this turned uglier. "Don't worry about him."

"Why do I have to defend myself?"

That night, we threw a back-to-class (and back-to-Trail) cookout. I will miss these friends, as I hike alone over the next nine hundred miles. Living with others is as much an adventure as slipping off a rock in Maine. Mark drove me to where I left the Trail, almost a two-hour roundtrip for him. As we shook hands, he said, "I would trade places with you in a second."

"No you wouldn't," I said.

Ranger Tom welcomed me back, but this time I did not stick around. Last week, when I left the Trail, it felt like summer. Now back, it feels like fall. I needed to head south – and fast. Since August began, I have spent more time taking off than hiking. On the other hand, I feel great and my boots are dry. Just another forty days to Springer Mountain, then it will all be over; all I must do is hike. Still, as I turned to watch Mark drive off, there were other places where I would rather be and other things I would rather do.

For much of the past month, whenever I left the Trail, I loved every minute being away. Did I come back because Mark wanted to hike alongside or because people like Craig were living their lives through me? Why did I come back other than I did not want to let everyone down, everyone whose sense of adventure was riding on me? My being at school so offended Craig and yet it was my last day before returning to the Trail. Now I am back. But he raised the question I have been asking, but the one I have been avoiding answering. Why do I hike? Is it so I can carry the burden of living the dreams of so many others, but one that was never mine? Am I stuck with a commitment I did not know I made, one that no longer makes any sense to me?

In the world with electricity, the setting sun provides a pleasurable moment of color. Now, back on the Trail, the sun defines my life. With so many miles to go, the seasons have changed and the daylight hours are shrinking. The sun was setting when I left the ranger station to hike into the woods. Daylight over a city street lasts a lot longer than under the canopy of trees. I figure it will take me fifty more days, if I limit my hiking to those hours when I can see the path before me.

I especially need to cover lots of miles now, before the equinox, and while I am still hiking on the smooth paths, through the national park. To reach Springer Mountain, I must hike without a break; no sightseeing, no days to recuperate. Just a commitment to the idea of finishing the Trail.

SEPTEMBER 13.

Rockfish Gap

So, here I am, sitting outside Howard Johnson's on Route 250. Why am I still getting blisters on my feet? How many more thousands of miles will I have to walk to get my feet hardened for hiking?

I started this hike with Rand, one of my best friends from college. We met during college orientation, when a bunch of us from the dorm went across the street to play basketball. I put on two pairs of socks and my high-top Adidas; he played in bare feet. I picked up my first blister hitchhiking from the Portland airport to Mt. Katahdin, and followed that with a never-ending supply. Rand, on the other hand, with feet as hardened as a goat, a veritable hiking machine, just walked and walked.

Although Rand was staying at the Anchorage when I called from Big Meadows, he took off the next day to continue his journey south before I got back to school. I guess he no more wanted to see me than I wanted to see him.

As I write, I am boiling spaghetti noodles on my portable Svea stove that I will eat alone in a gravel parking lot outside the Howard Johnsons, sitting a few yards from the pay phone.

In a while, I will call home, where my family has gathered to celebrate the Jewish New Year. My family eats traditional foods our ancestors picked up wandering through Eastern Europe, foods like gefilte fish, chopped liver, honey cake, and a round bread to symbolize the circle of life, the renewal of our lives. We also dip apples into honey to symbolize our wish for a sweet year.

Symbols like these are important reminders, but are not the central purpose of Judaism. Nor, for that matter, are the articles of faith, such as prayer and ritual. Those are the wrappers, not the substance; although if not for these wrappers, the Jewish people would not have lasted through thousands of years of persecution and exile. Nevertheless, Judaism is not defined by religious practice alone.

What is Judaism? Hillel, the sage, summed it up, saying "Simply to do unto others what you would have them do unto you – the rest is commentary." If they are called the "Chosen People," what were they chosen for? The answer is to serve as a guiding light for all the world, to make the world a better place. They are not on earth to rule it, to conquer it, or to convert it, but to live their lives morally and justly and to hope the rest of the world gets with the act.

The celebration of any New Year, regardless of the tradition, symbolizes renewal. It closes one book and opens another. Perhaps I should heed this lesson. Although I am presently surrounded by cars, not nature, there are many moments along the Trail, where the beauty is so intense it becomes easy to ascribe creation to a higher sense of intelligence, because random chance could not possibly have caused it all. I stopped earlier today in a forest, to eat some Gorp and drink some water. Looking around me, I saw granite stones splotched with lichen and dotted with moss. Growing around the rocks were ferns and then above them, small trees – pines and oaks – under a canopy of taller trees. A small brook made its way past where I sat, descending from the top of the Shenandoah to meet one of the rivers flowing east to the sea. Even the smell was heavenly: a clean mixture of smells, but with the hint of evergreen, wafted past me, subtle, but still there was a fragrance.

Then I stood up, shouldered my pack, and continued my solitary journey.

Last night, I slept on the grassy shoulder off Skyline Drive, about 25 miles south of Route 33, which was where I rejoined the Trail after my excursion to UVA. Something changed while I was away. The National Park returned to the animals. The crowds of people who squeezed into Big Meadows the week before, went home. The hundreds of people I passed each hour last week shrunk to tens, then ones. By late afternoon, I was alone.

The Trail took me along an abandoned orchard, no doubt

a relic from when the Shenandoah consisted of private farm-steads. The apples were small, because no one was there to thin the fruit; they were spotted, as no one sprayed them.

I tried one of the apples, carving out the bad spots with my pocket knife. They were tart but juicy, and so I picked a dozen, storing most in my pack, but I stuck a few into the nylon pocket on my shoulder strap.

I walked miles without seeing another person. I entered an oak forest and as I walked along an acorn covered path, I heard footsteps crunching from the forest. Twenty or so deer grazed nearby. My movements made them freeze, heads up, ready to run. I stood motionless. A sudden movement on my

part would send them bolting into the forest.

I heard a crunch behind me. I turned to face a young deer standing ten feet away. Small two-point antlers protruded from his head. Was he challenging my right to break his solitude or was he simply curious? He looked at me with neither fear nor malice, so I drew one of the small apples from the pocket on my strap and held it out in my hand. The deer's eyes focused on the apple and then he turned his head to look over to the herd. I continued to hold the apple. One step at a time, the young buck closed the distance between us. He took the apple in his mouth, carefully, without touching my skin, then turned to walk back toward the others. Two more young deer approached me.

"Okay, I have a few more apples left."

After that, the deer went back to grazing; I said goodbye and continued my journey south.

The sun set while I was still walking. When the Trail wound through fields or along the road, the stars and moon illuminated my steps. When I entered the forest, the trees blocked the light. I walked in the dark, illuminating my way with my tiny, space-saving, one triple-A battery flashlight. It was too dark to camp the required fifty feet off the Trail. Even if I could see, I could not be sure I would find a stretch of ground smooth enough to unroll my sleeping bag. Risking a ticket, I decided to make camp on the path. I flashed my light around to find an overhanging limb to string my pack out of the reach of bears. I unrolled my sleeping bag, slipped all the way in, covered my head, folded my arms over my chest, and fell asleep.

Sometime later, I was awakened, first by the sound, and then the feel of an animal walking up my sleeping bag. "Oh, my God," I thought, "there's a bear walking on me."

This was it, the moment I would be eaten – or mauled. I walked for over three months with no head butts from moose, no bear bashings, not even a snake licking. This was it. I lay there frozen, trying to think what to do, while keeping myself from breathing. I could feel the bear advancing up my body. What would be worse: being mauled by a bear or eaten by a bear? When it reached my chest I instinctively slammed my hands against the inside of the sleeping bag and sent the bear – or maybe it was a chipmunk or squirrel – sprawling into the brush, letting out a long stream of animal vituperative.

CHAPTER SIX

Courage

SEPTEMBER 14.

Go with the Flow

Last night, I ended my day staring over the Shenandoah Valley as the sun set and the stars filled the sky. The setting sun stretched lines of red and purple across the western sky. I slept peacefully on grassy stretches along the side of the road, while the evening breeze swept over my sleeping bag. The lights turned on in the hamlets and farms dotting the valley below. When the sun left the sky completely, I could not distinguish where the stars ended and the lights began.

I might just as easily have stopped a quarter mile sooner in the woods, but then I would have missed this lovely spot. Most days, I plan how far I will go, how many hours I will walk, and how fast I would have to walk each hour to reach my destination. Without scheduling like this, I would quit. My legs screamed for rest. Having a destination is one way to hike. The alternative is to walk until I feel like stopping.

There is a crew team that rows in water flowing east from this very same ridge. Although the University of Virginia perennially fields powerhouse teams in basketball and lacrosse, it leaves its Men's Crew team alone. Virginia has no Olympic oarsmen. It has simply a group of young men who keep themselves fit, while enjoying the changing seasons on the Rivanna River. They try to win races, but not at the expense of the rest of their lives. They are content to row the best races they have within themselves, even if that means riding in the other teams' wake. A plaque in their boathouse expresses their attitude, "Don't push the river. Just go with the flow."

Row within the best of your ability. Walk within the best of your ability. If I hiked three miles an hour for fifteen hours, I could travel forty-five miles a day. But some wildflowers are so small and delicate that they cannot be enjoyed unless the hiker bends way down to the ground and spends at least fifteen minutes watching the sun glisten off the colored petals.

There are people, Steve Jackson for instance, who can hike forty-five miles every day. I cannot. I must hike my hike; I must be me. All I can do is enjoy the world around me: the deer, the stars, and the flowers. Some people drive themselves to achieve records. Others drive themselves to reach the destination of their lifelong dream. And then, there is me: someone who has so much to live for in his life, so many wishes and desires. Yet, here I am still pushing to reach Georgia for an achievement that means nothing to me, on a hike I never wished to take. I walked from Maine to southern Virginia and yet all I can see is how far I have yet to travel. I told Dante Germino, the dean of my department at school, that hiking the first 2046 miles did not mean as much as hiking the last one. I wonder if he believed that or did he shake his head after I left his office.

As part of the orientation when I entered college, we read and discussed the book, *"Zen and the Art of Motorcycle Maintenance"* by Robert Pirsig; the cover of my book was purple. Pirsig wrote about taking family hikes during which his son would burst ahead, gaining satisfaction only from reaching the top of the mountain. The journey, Pirsig taught, was what mattered, not the destination. Because every journey we take, is really a journey of ourselves.

Maybe I would enjoy my life better if I could follow my own pace; hike for the moment; go with the flow. Eight oarsman and a coxswain can't be all wrong.

SEPTEMBER 15.

Laurel Spring

I have a lovely campsite near Laurel Spring. Not much of a view, but I am not looking. I am not walking either. I will not move another inch – ever again in my life – without my heart being into it.

I am one to trust my impulses. I did well on standardized tests even though I never checked my answers, because I believed my first answer was more likely to be correct than my second answer.

With the same impulsiveness, I agreed to go on this trek, not checking to see if this were the right thing for me, or if there could have been a Plan B for fulfilling my dream to study in England.

I was less impulsive when it came to preparing for the hike. I conducted research about equipment and how to handle food provisions, and yet, I decided on the most important decision of all, to go on the hike, in an instant, without a second thought, without wondering – "Why?" The problem, as I have learned, with climbing mountains head down, arms pumping, full speed ahead, is that sometimes we climb the wrong mountains.

So now, it has finally dawned on me to insist I answer the question "Why?" I already gathered enough information to decide whether to close this chapter of my life, but the days and miles kept going by long after I knew I should stop. Every part of my soul screams at me to move on with my life, yet I continue to walk south, placing goals like Hawk Mountain, Harper's Ferry, and Rockfish Gap as my conscious reasons to go on, to push me forward, so I could avoid making such an important decision. On and on I continue, not because I am fulfilling my dream, but because others may think less of me if I walk away. Maybe I will run for President of the United States, and my having completed the Trail, from start to finish, will attract enough voters to put me over the top. Maybe, one day, I will have a son and I will need to impress him by pointing to Maine on a map and then to Georgia and running my hand down in between.

What would standing atop Springer Mountain mean to me? I have been whittling away miles ever since that short-cut into Gorham. I skipped miles that I will never know were unpleasant or not. Maryland was a blur, because I traveled most of it in a series of car rides. No matter what I do from here, I can never claim to have hiked the exact 2,047 miles. I hope I never sink so low to claim that I hiked the whole thing. I may have added miles on side trails, but they do not offset the ones I missed.

When I set off for Maine, I was hiking the whole Trail – I declared as much. Just like at summer camp, when I was six years old, I declared: "I'm going to play third base, just like my Pop-Pop." Only this was not a single game. I have been at this for months and have so much time left before me.

A few days ago, while cooking spaghetti outside the Howard Johnson's, where Virginia highway 250 crosses the Blue Ridge Parkway, I thought about hitching into Charlottesville again. After only three days of hiking, I sported open sores along my back where the pack frame rubbed. What began as a cool September evening on top of Hightop Mountain turned again into enervating mugginess by the next day. I felt like a kid who keeps telling himself his life will get better when he turns sixteen, eighteen, twenty-one; always changing the age, but never doing anything to change his life.

I stopped wearing my hiking boots two days ago. During the week off in Charlottesville, they hardened into two bronze boats, just as heavy, but not quite as flexible. After three months of rain and mud, they could not withstand the dryness. After three trips to cobblers to replace the Vibram soles, uncountable waterproofings – and eleven states, I tied them to my pack. I walked from Black Rock Gap to Laurel Spring wearing the cheap pair of sneakers I bought to replace my lost moccasins. These offered no support, but compared to those boots, which have caused me three and a half months of pain, they have been a relief.

When I called home outside HoJo's, I told my father I hiked these last few days in a trance. I no longer think about all the things I want to learn, to do, and to achieve. I am just enduring. He said "You are young enough to try anything you wish, but you are old enough to make your own decisions – and you are too old to waste your life trying to please others."

I hiked a few more miles that night, unrolling my sleeping bag on the Trail after it became too dark to see. Once, I awoke with the light and fell asleep with the dark. Now, I awaken in the dark and go to sleep in the dark. I have hiked in the dark each of the past few days and, as the days grow shorter, I will spend even more hours of each day doing so.

That next morning I bathed in a creek, trying to cleanse my many open sores. I hiked the Trail in much the same manner I would have listened to a dull, unpleasant cellmate; I endured. At least in the Shenandoah, I could keep my head up while I walked. The paths there were wide and well maintained. The more typical trail – rock strewn and irregular – requires more concentration to avoid tripping.

While drinking from my canteen yesterday near Humpback Rocks, a yellow jacket stung me on my calf. There I was, just standing there, not bothering anyone: just some more gratuitous pain. Climbing down from the peak of Humpback Mountain, without the traction of Vibram soles, I slipped on some wet leaves, driving my knee against a boulder. Blood. If not for the pain, I wished I broke it. That would hand me an easy way out. These sneakers are not going to take me very far.

How can I stop hiking after I hiked so long? What would I tell all those people whom I told I would finish? Would I tell them, "After three and a half months I finally reached my destination and it turned out to be Laurel Spring?"

When I set out for Maine, I was looking for challenges. The Appalachian Trail fit that need. Although I could not clearly express it, I was looking for more than a long walk in the woods; I was searching for the key to controlling my life. I was tired of school year following school year, of not knowing where I was heading. It is not that I was failing in life; it is just that I was not striving toward anything that mattered. I felt I was drifting.

I did not come up with the burning passion to hike the Trail; I accepted an invitation to go along and it seemed like a good idea at the time. I was not in control of where I would stop each day; I selected my destination with a partner who then refused to hike together, so every destination was a compromise. This meant neither of us ever felt satisfied, so we broke apart to go our separate ways. It was only then that I began to control my daily routine. I alone determined where I would stop, or even whether I would walk at all. When faced with challenges, like reaching the Water Gap, I controlled when I awoke, and when I went to bed, along with every other detail on how I would reach those destinations. I no longer needed to compromise. I hiked independently, but nevertheless, I hiked alone. And alone was not how I want to live my life.

My reason for hiking was not to reach Springer Mountain, but to learn how to take responsibility for my life, and that goes back to when I first stuck my thumb out on I-95 in Maine. And despite the blisters that formed even before reaching Katahdin, and the many that followed, I continued to search. Each day I put on my boots, reached scenic overlooks, passed dismal swamps, and entered towns, some beautiful and some not so beautiful. I hiked for serenity; I hiked to overcome physical challenges; but mostly, I hiked to find a life that seemed lost. Prior to the Trail, I was squandering the dream of my youth, not the one of becoming a Mouseketeer – no, not that dream – but the dream of becoming a man of passion, of drive, of meaning: someone I could respect. A man like my father, who defines his life not by money, but by the difference he makes on the world around him.

A life worth living is not about the job title and certainly not about the income. A successful person starts each day aligned with who he is. The Trail has taught me I can rely on my wits and my personal strength. I can climb when too weary; I can withstand the ugly ordeal of putting heavy boots on feet covered with blisters. I can face a double blaze and turn right —and, if need be, turn around and hike left. I can suffer the cold, dampness, bugs of all shapes and sizes, and not give in to fear or allow despair to overwhelm me to the point of inaction. If I can take the energy I spent climbing Katahdin, I could succeed at school, my job, my life.

Someday, I will recall these days of hunger and thirst to apply the same endurance to the hardships I will face during my life. I will learn to be thankful for the abundance around me – running water, mattresses, windows with screens – which I have hitherto taken for granted. Sure, I will seem strange, maybe even annoying, when I shout "Look, running water," but that too shall pass.

My dad did not leave high school and say, "I know what I will do for the rest of my life." During World War II, his choice was between the Army or the Navy. Nor did he know what would happen after law school. The jobs did not define him. It was the passion he brought to these jobs, in his case, to right wrongs, to teach others how to speak for themselves and to become full American citizens. The path he took through life was hardly smooth, but it was guided by a common purpose, so he was always able to treat his triumphs and disasters just the same.

What have I learned from the Trail and am I ready to move on? I followed Katahdin with Chairback, and Chairback with Bigelow, and then Bigelow with Mahoosuc. At the start, I was focused on reaching Springer Mountain, the goal, the destination of any worthwhile Southbounder. But was any of that my

dream or was it Rand's? My dream was to do something different, to shake my life from my stupor, to start me on my real
journey. I know now a few hundred more miles with a pack
on my back will not finish the job. I proved that any journey is
just a long series of steps. There are days when those steps will
falter; even some spent headed in the wrong direction. The
challenge is to keep moving forward, because I am not in this
to reach a final destination like Springer Mountain, but to live
the rest of my life heading in the right direction.

Seated just a few feet from Laurel Spring, I scribbled these
notes into my journal, occasionally filling my Sierra Cup with
water. Of all the gear I took with me, this cup has proven the
most dependable. It is one of the few pieces of gear I did not
lose along the way.

I have so many ideas for what comes next with my life,
the things I want to do, the places I want to see, and the great
things I hope to accomplish. For the first time in my life, I
realize that dreams really can come true, provided we do some
planning, make some preparations (like mailing food to post
offices along the way), buy a few pieces of reliable and essential
equipment, and then place one foot in front of the other.

I need nobody's permission to hike or to stop. I bear the
consequences of my success or failure. I know now I do not
hike to seek my parent's approval or to earn their love. They
have said over and over that I have both unconditionally and
that this journey is for me and me alone. My friends who
matter accept me for who I am, not for what I do; those that
don't – don't matter. Everyone else is a mere spectator.

I wish I could say I finished the Appalachian Trail, but I
no longer want to hike it. I wish I could say I hit the home
run that won the World Series for Philadelphia, but that is not

going to happen either. The past few weeks have already been a denial of what I have learned. Racing another hundred miles to Snowden, Virginia, to pick up another week's worth of meals is not on the list of things I want to do with my life. In fact, picking up that package would be a violation of everything I want in life. If there is something worth doing, from now on, I want to do it with all my heart and with every ounce of energy I can muster. And if it is not worth doing, then I won't do it. The time I have left in my life is fleeting. I will not waste it hanging on to someone else's dream, because others might think me a failure or a dope for having gotten involved with it in the first place. Okay, I am a dope – now I am moving on.

The hike was never about reaching Springer Mountain; I realize that now. There were many Thru-hikers who reach the base of Katahdin, but never get to climb it; it was random chance that enabled us to show up on a day when nature and the rangers allowed us to climb the mountain. Nevertheless, they were still Thru-hikers. So many intended to hike the whole thing. But not one Thru-hiker allowed the fear of not being able to complete the whole Trail stop them from trying.

And so it goes; for me, there are too many things I would rather do than spend another month or two hiking the Trail. I climbed Katahdin. I battled the black flies, the rain, the starvation and the thirst. I crossed the mud of Maine and the rocks of Pennsylvania and now, here I am in southern Virginia. I faced all the dangers, the discomforts, the physical tests and yet, of all the challenges facing me on the Appalachian Trail, the biggest challenge of all has been to turn and walk away.

ACKNOWLEDGEMENTS

Thank you to all those who helped make this book successful, from those who helped me along the actual journey years ago, to those who first printed my articles in the weekly paper, *The Declaration*, to those who helped guide me to put these pages together in the format that made sense.

Thank you to my wife Julia Grant Barol for her unfailing support in the writing of these books. Without her, this never would have happened. Thank you to Aimerie Hallowell, for her edits and other contributions. Thank you to Galen Rebecca McMullen, Judith Morris, and to Jada Byrd for turning the words into images.

Thank you to my many friends and to the many strangers who helped me, were kind to me, and who extended their best wishes. Thank you to Simon Acheson, my first roommate in college, who helped me more than he will know. Special thanks to our next-door neighbor, J. Mark Klamer, who as Editor-in-Chief of *The Declaration*, published my first articles, which formed the basis for these books. And thank you to his roommate, Rand Elmquist, who invited me to join him in pursuit of his lifelong dream. It may not have been what I would have chosen to do, but it certainly influenced how the rest of my life turned out.

Rand continued to hike past Charlottesville until he finished the entire Trail. Although we lived in the same house, the Anchorage, for the remainder of our Third Year, and saw each other through the remainder of college, we never talked about the Trail ever again.

DISCUSSION QUESTIONS

The main character searches for something. What is it?

Was the main character better served hiking or leaving the Trail?

How has your culture, friends, family, religion shaped the choices you make in life?

West Mt. Airy avoided the extreme polarizations that swept communities all over the country in the Sixties and Seventies. Why did it remain calm and stable and what lessons could others use?

Have you stayed at something too long? Have you quit too early? How did you know the difference?

What role do animals play in your life? Are you a hunter for food or for sport? Do you fear animals? Do they give you energy?

Have you found yourself searching for the cause of your feelings of sadness, loneliness, or depression? How much of this was internal and how much of it was due to a burden you carried? How did you shed that burden?

The main character's father influenced his life in many ways. Did he allow his image of his father to constrain his choices? Do we allow ourselves to project expectations of others that are not there?

What is meant by: "If I am not for myself, who will be; if I am only for myself, what am I; if not now, when"?

Notes From The Trail
Book One

(Excerpt)

The
Long Green
Tunnel

David Barol

WARNING!!

Do not pick up this book if you want to read something on hiking. This is not the book for you. Put — the Kindle — back.

This is no more a book on hiking than *Huckleberry Finn* was a book on boating. Sure, Huck Finn had something to do with a river — but that is not the point.

Notes from the Trail starts with the promise of great adventure. After flying to Maine, two young men reached Mt. Katahdin to begin their journey south along the Appalachian Trail. Okay, so far it sounds like hiking.

As an aside, now more than 3,000 people annually attempt to hike the entire Appalachian Trail, either from south to north or from north to south. Walking twenty miles a day, every day, just for a week, sounds exhausting. Extending that pace to one hundred straight days still won't get you to the other end. Who in their right mind would want to do such a thing?

Each person who begins such a quest — and this includes all the other journeys such as the Pacific Crest Trail or El Camino de Santiago in Spain — soon realizes the challenge is not the length they must walk or the heights they must climb. Rather, it is the journey they must take in their own mind. Many who start soon learn that the journey is not so much physical as it is metaphysical. Three quarters of those who begin the Appalachian Trail stop before the end, many limping away in pain, some running out of time, but there are others who find what they came for, having reached the destination that matters most.

This book touches a bit on adventure and blisters, vistas and mud, but it explores so much more than a trail. It explores a young man's journey in search of his dream. For without his dream to guide him, he wandered into a five-month walk in the woods aimlessly following the dream of his friend.

Who knew hiking partners would go through the same ups and downs as married couples? We fall in love with the idea of a future together but we fear ruining the courtship by digging beneath the surface. Just so we are clear: this is no more a book on relationships than it is a book about hiking, but what goes on between these two young men shapes the story.

This trip will forever mark these two young men. There are defining moments for all of us that measure how we grow from one stage of our lives to another. For my father, one such moment came while visiting his aunt on a Sunday in December, 1941. My first such moment came when I was six, looking at the news from Dallas. The picture I remember most is the fallen President's little boy saluting the funeral procession. As I got older, I remember watching the national draft on television, lotteries from which nobody emerged a winner.

I can tell you where I was when I heard the first footsteps on the moon; I even looked up. And I remember my eighteenth birthday, when the news showed those frantic people scrambling to board the last helicopter leaving the roof of the US Embassy in Saigon before the Viet Cong entered the compound and brought the Viet Nam war to a close.

That era shaped me, but mine are the eyes of a generational in-betweener. The requirement to register for the draft ended a month before it was my turn. We were the younger siblings: too young to fight in Viet Nam, march on Washington, or get down at Woodstock. We saw the body counts, bra burnings, and sexual revolution on the news, but we most likely did so because we had turned on the television early so as not to miss the beginning of *Gilligan's Island*.

I fall between the Viet Nam generation and those younger, for whom Viet Nam and the Sixties were historical events, for whom the chase of the White Bronco means something but the connection between Roosevelt Grier and Bobby Kennedy, not so much.

I grew up amongst so much change I thought change was normal. I lived in the fourth largest city in America and attended public schools. I was a white kid in a school district that turned increasingly integrated with each passing year. I witnessed the turmoil caused by the frustration of segregation, the murder of Martin Luther King, and with the mutual distrust of the police. The dynamics that played out colored my impressions of people and influenced what I consider important.

Although the Sixties affected me, and the city influenced me, my parents raised me. They believed in the power of a community action to change lives and they viewed the community as the foundation of the great nation we could be, a nation in which all its people embodied the sacred ideals on which it was founded. My parents worked with passion to keep our neighborhood from disintegrating like so many others. They did not turn and run, but rather they greeted newcomers with an outstretched hand and integrated them into their lives.

My father's search for meaning led him to the words expressed most elegantly by our third president, Thomas Jefferson. During a summer trip, he and my mother visited the University of Virginia where they signed me up for an admissions packet. Both the university Jefferson created, and the man himself, influenced me and, in turn, this book.

You can see already that *The Long Green Tunnel*, the first book in the *Notes From The Trail* series, is not a book about how to rub two sticks together. It searches for dreams, both that of the books' storyteller, and for the rest of us, the American Dream.

I am not saying that stories about flies, swamps, and mountain ledges are not important. Perhaps these were the challenges this young man needed to head him in the right direction. If, despite all the warnings, you still want a book on hiking, you will find some rocks to climb and tents to pitch inside. And, did you hear the one about the moose?

Let me be perfectly clear about the time and place. The book starts in Maine in 1977. The storyteller keeps a journal, writing about what took place each day. The present takes place as he is writing. What took place ten minutes earlier was the past and what he anticipated eating in a few minutes is the future — even though that too happened a long time ago, when our country still had a king, when we were briefly fighting no wars, and when our President addressed the nation looking like Mr. Rogers.

That's a bit about what you have in store. It is a journey. It takes place along a trail. But it definitely is not a book about hiking.

—DAVID BAROL

CHAPTER ONE

Optimism

JUNE 1, AM

Abol Campground, Baxter State Park

We left Philadelphia yesterday at 7:37 aboard a Boeing 737. After switching planes in Boston, we arrived in Bangor, Maine. It was my first flight and my first holding pattern. In two and a half hours we travelled 700 miles; in the next four, we travelled ten. I learned already that flying beats hitchhiking.

When I made the plane reservations, the ticket agent asked, "Shall I book a return ticket?"

"Nah, don't bother," I said, "I'll walk back."

I guess she did not get many calls from Appalachian Trail hikers, although I am not an official one yet. I won't earn that distinction until later today.

What joy it will be to hike every day under these blue New England skies and the bright but not overly warm sun. In a few minutes, Rand, my hiking partner and I will leave our campsite to climb Mount Katahdin, the highest mountain in

Maine. We could see Katahdin from fifty miles away, looming large and solitary against the sky. Tomorrow we will begin our journey south to Georgia, although Katahdin will continue to loom over our shoulders for days to come.

I am here because Rand asked me. We have been great friends since the first day of college, at the University of Virginia. It was an honor to be the one person he wanted to go with on this great adventure. We are so alike. Both Eagle Scouts, we get the job done without having to be asked and we both desire to get the job done right. We are a hand and a glove, a pair of bookends, a hot dog and a bun — perfectly matched and identically suited to hike the Appalachian Trail.

JUNE 1, PM

Katahdin Stream Campground

Now, then; that wasn't so bad. Yeah, right.

It took us nine hours to climb Katahdin in what has been the most exhausting day of my life. Fortunately, the ranger drove our packs from last night's campground to this one, so we did not have to carry them up and over that beast.

We started the day walking on a path that began to rise and fall but never falling as much as it rose. Within minutes, Rand and I stood mesmerized by an amazing sight: a blow-down where hundreds of trees leaned one against the other. From where we stood, we could see an entire valley of green trees surrounding a huge swath of grey dying wood and barren soil.

Rand asked me to help him pursue his lifelong dream of hiking the Appalachian Trail. Intelligent and introspective, I never once heard him say an unkind word to anyone.

That was before today.

As we stared in awe at the blowdown, he said something that left me speechless. I would rather not write it down as I hope to shake it off. I know if I dwell on it, I will make it worse. Like water on a duck's back, I will let this drip off, besides, it was the only cloud on an otherwise sunny day.

After saying his piece, he abruptly left. I hiked alone for the next hour. When I broke through the treeline I could see the horizon far to the east. I nearly caught up with Rand as we scrambled up a field of rocks. Ahead, I saw the top of the mountain and the beginning of the AT. I pressed on without pause. Pulling myself onto what I thought was the top of the mountain, I gaped at what looked like another mountain left to climb.

I had reached the summit, not the peak. I walked on, passing a sign that read "Thoreau's Spring," but there was no water, which may explain why Thoreau went crazy hiking in Maine. Henry David Thoreau travelled this way more than a century ago, then wrote about it. I will try to write about Maine while holding on to my sanity.

In a mile I reached Baxter Peak, where I touched the sign that marked the start of the Appalachian Trail, making me official. I turned south and, from then on, walked on the Appalachian Trail, the 2,100 mile footpath that will take me from Maine to Springer Mountain. I became a Southbounder, not to be confused with those other Thruhikers known as Northbounders, who will invade these woods in a few weeks after their migration north from Georgia.

Climbing Katahdin was hard; climbing down was treacherous. I lowered myself from one granite ledge to another. Looking left or looking right made no difference: looking in either direction meant looking straight down. Holding onto one ledge to drop to another gave me the sense that I was one slip from falling. I inched out from one ledge and then dropped to the ledge below, fighting the image that I could easily bounce off a rock and fall over the side. From looking out from such heights, I could see how someone thought up infinity.

I heard about people who became so frightened they stuck to their ledge, not budging until other hikers guided them down. One such rescuer helping an older gentleman, slipped, and broke his own leg.

Rand and I descended without incident and found our packs at the ranger station. We slept under the stars in an empty campsite. Tomorrow, it all begins.

JUNE 2

Hurd Lean-to

Unlike the blue sky of yesterday, today it rained off and on. Both my feet felt as if I dropped them into a creek, which, in fact, I did. After that misadventure, I changed the dressings on my feet, put on dry socks, and continued walking. But the wet bushes, the dripping trees, and the muddy trail soaked my shoes so within minutes both feet were sloshing wet once again.

At the end of the day, when I arrived at the Hurd Lean-to, I was greeted by a chorus of "Welcome, Thruhiker!"

I walked my first complete day on the Appalachian Trail, having touched the marker on top of Mt. Katahdin yesterday. I am a Thruhiker. Next stop: Springer Mountain.

A lean-to is a small building with three sides and a sloped roof. Although Hurd Lean-to must be twenty feet across, it feels crowded. My partner was the fourth to arrive and I made number five. Three more came from the south, having walked all week. The two who greeted me hail from Texas.

They had hiked north from Monson, Maine, with the hope of climbing Katahdin. After that they will hitchhike to New Hampshire for a week in the White Mountains; it will take us a month to walk there.

The other guy who arrived before me hoped to climb Katahdin today, but the rangers closed the mountain because of the rain. What a difference one day makes. Rather than risk waiting endlessly at the base of the mountain, he began his hike towards Georgia, figuring he could come back to climb Katahdin some other year. It seems a shame to miss the start of the Trail after going through so much effort just to reach the base of the great mountain.

He is a tall, thin guy with sandy hair and a tiny blue pack. I cannot imagine he has much in the way of food in there. He pitched his blue one-man tent away from the lean-to and stayed by himself. Not having climbed Katahdin disqualifies him as an official Thruhiker so he can keep his distance.

The Texas guys are well-seasoned hikers who use many of the skills they learned in Viet Nam. They pack light and carry cooked rice which they eat hot or cold. They told us not to salt our food because salt is "bad for your health"; instead they carried miso paste, the fermented soybean concentrate that has "a tenth the sodium of salt." We carry salt tablets with us in case of dehydration and yet these two told us we eat too much salt.

I read books on hiking, most notably the one written by Colin Fletcher, the Patron Saint of backpackers. My partner, Rand, and I are both Eagle Scouts, so we know our way around a backpack. We planned and organized everything perfectly.

After all this work, my head is so full that one more suggestion would cause it to burst.

❧ ❧ ❧

I moved away from the lean-to to keep writing as those two make me feel deflated. They just warned that we "are in for a week of mud and mosquitoes; you don't know what you've got yourselves in for." Then they told me my pack is too heavy; I will not need all the clothing I packed, and I will never have time to read the half dozen books I carry with me.

Well, at least I climbed Katahdin.

Today, there were plenty of chances to read. I walked a total of ten miles, all by myself, and although I am tired, it did not take much time. It rained most of the day but I enjoyed the few breaks when the sun broke through the overcast sky. I found a log or rock to sit upon or a tree to lean against so I could continue to read *One Flew over the Cuckoo's Nest* by Ken Kesey. I am so into the book I can pick up the story no matter where I left off. Although, I am not sure where Kesey is coming from, whether he wants to expose the conditions in mental hospitals or wants to point out the abuse of the insanity plea, he sure knows how to tell a good story. I feel enclosed in the mental ward as I read this book even though I am reading it in a forest without walls.

The Trail south of Katahdin wound through a dense thicket of trees along brooks and streams. There were no scenic over-looks, just a never ending wood. For most of the walk, I could not see the sky as the trees on either side of the path met just above my head. I saw no views but instead walked inside a long, green tunnel.

I crossed a road at the southern edge of Baxter State Park, which the guidebook declared was the last hard paved road before entering the "100 Mile Wilderness," a Tolkien name if ever there was one. Although I left first, my hiking partner passed me and remained out of sight for the rest of the day. Since there was no one to share my thoughts or observations with, I read. Not a problem, really, as I am an unrepentant Marxist. It was Groucho who said, "Outside of a dog, a book is man's best friend; inside a dog, it's too dark to read."

I thought of a thousand different ideas as I walked, but like a night's dreams, I can barely remember any of them. So I decided to jot my thoughts on a paper whenever I pause so I can transfer them to these pages each night. So, if I do go insane like Thoreau, my biographers — or psychoanalysts — can mark the exact moment.

JUNE 3

Rainbow Stream Lean-to

Here we are at the Rainbow Stream Laundromat. That is how it looks with all the multi-colored shirts, towels, and socks hanging from the rafters. The sky is grey and the air cold but after two days of it, I expect no more rain.

The lean-to overlooks a stream with water just warm enough to soak my blistered feet. The blisters are not healing because my feet are wet all the time.

Nevertheless, I found my pace today. There is no greater joy than to roll along, uphill and down. Despite the rolling pace, the hiker should refrain from becoming too ecstatic about his good days for then it follows he will become overwhelmed by the bad. A bad week in Maine and we will find our lonely hiker

standing along the highway holding a sign that reads: "Home."
Separate the emotion from the walking — that's what I say —
take it all in stride. Walking should be the means to see beauty;
for if you are into the beauty of walking, then you run the risk
of being overwhelmed by the ugliness as well.

Rand and I have our own approach to hiking together. We
don't. In fact, we never hike within one hundred yards of each
other: far enough for each hiker to feel alone; far enough for
swinging branches to come to rest; for red packs to disappear;
for mother ruffed grouses to become unruffled. Still it seems
strange to hike the Trail with someone and not see him.

I guess I will get used to it.

JUNE 4

Nahmakanta Lake Lean-to

I am sitting by the tent waiting for Rand to focus his camera in
the setting light. In a few moments, the quiet guy from Michigan
will take a picture of us pretending to study a map. I have
now spent three nights with this guy but have exchanged a
total of ten words. He set up his tent in the woods, far from
ours, and kept to himself. He will leave after the picture but
we will share a campsite with him again tonight at a spot some
twelve miles away.

There were two good reasons why we pitched a tent by
a lean-to. The first was that the lean-to lacked a platform and
the mud floor looked like a pig sty. The second was that at
every turn, we were enveloped by clouds of buzzing insects
— black flies and mosquitoes — forcing us to spend our time
zipped inside our tent. The flies were tiny little black things,
not much bigger than gnats. They swarmed but did not land.

The mosquitoes showed no such inhibitions. They landed at will and my face has the welts to prove it.

My tale of woe does not end with my face. I got blisters within an hour of landing in Maine. I am like a soldier just landed in Saigon who gets hit crossing the tarmac by a jeep. I got my blisters trying to thumb a ride one hundred miles south of Kathadin.

Each morning, I wash the blisters with Dr. Bronner's Peppermint Soap to get the dirt out. After the foot has dried, I apply an antibacterial ointment, next, a Band-Aid, followed by moleskin, all of which I wrap with adhesive tape. The moleskin reduces the friction between the tender spots and the boot, thus making it possible to walk without crippling pain. I still feel pain, especially when I start in the morning, but it is not crippling. I told Rand that with the blister, the heavy pack, and the rough terrain, I have found it difficult to find my pace. "I can cope with two out of the three," I said, "but not all three at once." And so I delude myself.

I carry my healing supplies in a small bag in the lower left pocket of my pack. The clever people who designed my pack built it into two sections, with multiple pockets, so I do not have to rummage to reach stuff. I store items of a similar function in nylon bags. If I need my flashlight, I can touch my pack, move my hand to the top right pocket, find the zipper and reach in. Matches are in the same pocket, with the rest of my emergency gear like my compass and whistle. My poncho always gets rolled and stored in the bottom section of the pack, so even if I have the rain cover on, all I have to do is uncover the bottom section and pull it out. A place for everything and everything in its place. This morning, about two miles into the hike, I reached the Pollywog Stream Ford. A "ford" is just another name for "there is no bridge." Pollywog is a wide stream with a fast current, filled with water that was melting snow only a few moments before.

Rather than ruin my first aid by walking across the stream, I came up with a solution worthy of Thomas Jefferson. My partner and I met at the University of Virginia, Mr. Jefferson's University, which remains a living museum to the ingenuity, the love of learning and design, and to the civility of this great man. He filled his home at Monticello with his clever ideas, not unlike my backpack.

I carried the plastic trash bag the ranger gave us in Baxter State Park with the warning, "You packed it in; you can pack it out." I stuck my bandaged foot into the bag and pulled the drawstrings taut. I next wrapped my nylon rain chaps around the top of the bag forming an airtight seal. Then I carefully stepped across the stream. What a sight I must have been. With a giant pack on my back, two boots in one hand, I stepped gingerly across the bone-chilling creek with my other hand clutching the drawstring of — a — bag — filled — with water.

I have so let Jefferson down.

This hike is about more than trees and mountains. I am walking a trail that winds through the pathways of my mind. I am going to make a habit of writing something each day without fail.

JUNE 6

The Old Logging Camp

Yesterday started innocently enough with the three of us planning to meet at the Old Logging Camp, which the guidebook placed twelve miles south of where we started and 1.7 miles past the Old Stag Antlers Camp. The quiet guy left first while Rand walked to the lake to supplement the two brook trout a fisherman gave us, using the hook and line he packed. He came up short but sautéed the two trout on the Svea stove.

After eating our pack food for three days, I relished every bite of these fish that lived their lives in Nahmakanta Lake. The water was clear, cold, and inviting; the only way to get there was by walking the Appalachian Trail or taking the gravel jeep road through lands owned by the Great Northern Paper Company. You can taste the fresh mountain lake with every bite.

As I was eating, a friendly — although odd smelling — Malamute padded over. I gave the dog's cheeks a shake then looked at my hands. He had been sniffing at our privy, which was nothing more than a branch nailed across two stumps.

"Let's go boy," I said.

I washed my hands in the lake, which deserved better. Stopping by the truck of the fishermen who gave us the trout, I ordered the dog to stay. When I returned to the site there he was to greet me, wagging his tail.

It started to rain so Rand went back into the tent to read while I took off, walking the first five miles along the gravel road. The guidebook called this stretch the "100 Mile Wilderness." There are some roads made of gravel and some just of mud, but for the most part, we hike along dirt paths cut through forests. And, falling upon whatever surface we have walked, has been the rain that has accompanied us since we left Katahdin.

I did not invite the dog along, but along he came. Instead of following me, he led me, with his tongue lolling to the side. He stayed fifty feet in front occasionally looking back to make

sure I was still there. I yelled for him to go home but each time
I did, he would run further ahead. His fur was black and white
but his eyes were as blue as the sky, not the sky I could see in
Maine, but somewhere. He was solidly built with a full coat of
fur and obviously had been well-cared for.

For two hours he trotted in front of me, occasionally falling behind to follow a scent, but always racing ahead. Strange,
but this has been the closest I have come to actually hiking
with someone since entering Maine.

How great it would be to hike the Trail with a dog like him.
He was so full of spirit he almost danced when he ran. I imagined him sitting next to me by the campfire and curling against

me at night, adding an extra body's heat for these cold, rainy nights. A malamute is a dog born to pull a sled, which explains why he felt it necessary to run in front of me, looking back, laughing to himself about how he anointed himself the lead dog. I guess I helped him self-actualize.

After two hours of brisk walking, I saw the double blazes signaling a change of direction. The Trail left the gravel road and cut into the woods. I stopped. The dog kept walking but when he turned to look for me, I ran toward him. He sprung in the air and raced as fast as he could. When I reached the turnoff, I lunged into the high grass and crawled behind a tree. A few moments later, he galloped past, thinking I playfully ran the five miles back to the lake.

I felt bad for tricking him but hoped Rand would think to do the same. This was the most beautiful dog in the world but he belonged to somebody and I could not take such a magnificent animal. If I allowed him to follow me that would be tantamount to stealing and, if I put myself into his owner's boots, I could not imagine losing such a great dog.

Anyone setting out on such an adventure needs to decide upon a moral code and then realize that circumstances will test that resolution. During our first week at Virginia, we signed pledges to support the student run Honor System, which tolerates neither lying, cheating, nor stealing. After high school, where there had been plenty of lying, cheating, and stealing, I found it refreshing to go through college knowing that the teachers compared my best efforts with the best efforts of others, without the fear of falling behind those who were getting ahead by cheating.

My partner and I shared a house with ten other guys. None of us had locks on our doors. Although I did not have much worth stealing, I never had so much as a pencil taken from me. But we are many miles away from The University and its Honor System. Can we now lie, cheat and steal? Does what happens on the Trail, stay on the Trail?

I would never take another person's dog, Honor System or no Honor System. Maybe he belonged to the fishermen but not finding them by their truck figured they had abandoned him; all the while they were sitting in their boat in the middle of the lake. Conversely, what if someone drove into the back country, let him out, and then drove off hoping to save on dog food bills. In that case, sticking with us might be his only way to survive. I may have left a domesticated dog to die because of my over developed concern over honor. I can hear my father's warning, "Justice tempered with mercy."

After pulling a fast one on the malamute, I entered a grove of saplings. I kept thinking about the dog, hoping I did the right thing. At least if he did not belong to the fishermen, they would realize that the dog's fate lay with them and they could drive him to safety.

After an hour, I reached the Potaywadjo Lean-to. I figured my partner would reach me any minute; he walked so much faster and he did not have blisters. According to the guide-book, the spring by the lean-to is the "largest and coldest in all Maine" and is "A joy to the hiker." They were not kidding: the water tasted sweet and cold. Bubbles gurgled from the white sandy bottom just as they would from a water cooler. After drinking my fill, I moved on; the mosquitoes were thirstier than I.

Three miles farther, I came upon the ruins of the Old Antler's Camp on the Lower Jo-Mary Lake. I could stop just for a moment to look at the abandoned buildings; the mosquitoes drove me on. This camp, and many more like it, flourished for years as hunting and fishing camps in the Maine Woods. You could fly to these camps by seaplane as they all sit on the shores of clear pristine lakes. But for the most part, the camps have disappeared, decaying into the wilderness. In fact, it seems that most of Maine has returned to its primordial state. I have walked along stone walls holding back trees and mud from meeting other trees and mud. Maine is one of the few places with fewer people on the land today than the century before.

Judging from the guidebook, I was still two miles from the "Old Logging Camp." I figured that when I reached the camp, I would join the quiet hiker in his blue tent to avoid the mosquitoes. Maybe there would be some old cabins or a dining hall, something to mark the spot.

I was getting weary. The mosquitoes ignored the rain and forced me to keep moving, blanketing my hands and face whenever I stopped. I smeared my face with Old Woodsman bug repellent — scented with that distinctive smell of tar — ignoring the price I would one day pay with brain damage.

I moved on, surprised my partner had not reached me. On the other days, although I left first, he passed me within the first few hours. I would hear his footsteps and sense him walking behind me. I would quicken my pace but he would continue to gain on me. Then, if the path widened or my step faltered, he would pass me and keep going without a word or a wave.

I kept walking, occasionally stopping to look at the map. I saw neither the blue tent nor anything that resembled an old logging camp. And yet, given the time since my last landmark, I should easily have travelled the distance. The trouble was, I did not know what a new logging camp looked like, let alone an old logging camp.

I crossed the mouth of Mud Pond on a series of submerged logs and then inched along a birch sapling that someone laid from one bank to the other of a nearby stream. It wobbled up and down so fast I would have fallen into the rushing water had I not jumped back to shore. Perplexed, I looked upstream for a crossing. I crossed several streams in Maine — few with bridges. This would not normally pose a challenge but with all the rain, the water funneling through the banks made the crossing dangerous. Twenty yards upstream, I could see how I might hop from rock to rock. As usual, I slipped and fell in.

At least I was not getting any wetter. In the clearings, the drenching rain drove me on; in the woods, the droning mosquitoes kept me from stopping. It was raining too hard to read but I paused several times to give Rand the chance to catch up. The sky grew darker; I walked on.

I came upon a large fallen tree that blocked my path. I faced three choices. Either I could climb over it, or I could squeeze under it, or I could walk around it. Colin Fletcher in his *Complete Backpacker* advised us to walk around rather than step over and step over that which you cannot walk around — but never step on a fallen tree lest you slip.

I thought it strange that Rand had not passed me. I had already walked more miles than on any other day. I looked for either the old lumber camp or the blue tent of the silent hiker.

Then I came to the Great Northern Paper Company Road which crossed the Trail by Cooper Falls. I looked down at the yellow gravel brimming with water from the driving rain. From where I stood, I could not see the falls but after a day of walking in silence, the roar of the water jarred me. The old logging camp was two miles back, but I saw neither a blue tent nor any evidence of a camp of any sort. And where was Rand?

It was hours and now fifteen miles since I last saw him; it was unlike him to lag behind.

A jeep passed; I waved. I read the wooden milepost: "14.5 miles north to Lake Nahmakanta Lean-to, 4 miles north to Jo-Mary Lake; 3.8 miles south to Cooper Falls Shelter. I pulled my watch out of my pack. It was quarter to six.

I felt the rising flame of panic. The three of us were supposed to camp over two miles back, but I could swear on the Bible, if I carried one, that nothing resembled a camp, let alone a camper. What if the silent hiker, in an effort to find dry ground, pitched his tent well off the Trail? Maybe I missed him. I did not know what to do, but figured walking south was pointless. If the silent hiker continued to the next lean-to that was his decision; my concern was with my partner.

Suppose something happened to him; suppose he slipped while stepping on a fallen tree and broke his leg; perhaps he had not read Colin Fletcher's book. Visions of death now surfaced in my mind. I saw him lying face down in a stream. I saw myself lifting him up, his eyes bulging, his stiff arm pointing at me.

I needed to go back. I leaned my pack against a tree, put on my poncho, and reached into the "emergency pocket" to collect my whistle, pen knife, signal mirror, waterproof match case, and compass. I set off to find the others. But after a half-mile, I scolded myself for panicking — if I missed the lumber camp so maybe did the silent hiker, and Rand would certainly keep walking until he found me. I sat down on a log and tried to shake my head clear of panic, realizing I was in no condition to man a search. I overshot the mark by 2.3 miles, but what about the other hiker? Why did my partner not catch up? I returned to the gravel road.

I blew my whistle three times. Silence. Or rather, the incessant roar of the nearby falls and the constant pelting of the rain. I panicked once more. I knew I was alive; I had no recollection dying. And I figured I could continue the hike alone if need be. But what could have happened? How could my partner not have reached me? It was almost 6:30 and I was still alone. Rand does not take leisurely walks; he is a walking machine. Even when he spots me five miles, he passes me by noon.

I needed to calm my nerves, reduce my anxiety. I wished I could call my father. I did not know what to do and I needed to rely on someone with real experience. I put my poncho over my head and sought the calming influence of my book, *One Flew over the Cuckoo's Nest*, but my glasses kept fogging and the blue light that seeped through the poncho made reading difficult. "Enough of this," I said aloud. "I have to do something."

It was 6:45. I was hungry, tired, and thoroughly wet and cold. I knew I would weaken if I did not take care of myself and get out of the rain. I would have to make camp in the rain without the tent, the one piece of community equipment my partner carried.

What would Jefferson do? My poncho came with brass grommets at each corner and I carried a ground cloth. I packed one hundred feet of rope. Looking for a place to set up camp, I found a level piece of ground overlooking the falls. I tied a length of rope between two trees thinking I could lay my ground cloth over it and secure the four corners to the ground, sort of like a pup tent, but the mathematics let me down: a four by eight foot tarp, turned into an equilateral triangle has a base just two feet wide, not enough to shield a sleeping bag from the rain. It takes a lot more material to make a pup tent than I originally thought.

Again I asked, "What would Jefferson do?" I undid the rope and ran it through the two grommets at one end of my poncho. I then cut two more pieces of rope, running each from the remaining two corners to the bases of nearby trees. Instead of a pup tent, I created a lean-to, which covered an area four feet wide and about seven feet long, losing about a foot in length because of the thirty degree slope. It would keep me dry if I could solve two complications. Nothing kept the top of the poncho from bunching together and most lean-tos do not have a hole in the middle for a head to pop through.

The hood problem was easily remedied by pulling the drawstrings taut. Only when I did so, I pulled so hard that I ripped the draw strings out of the lightweight nylon hood. The less destructive method for closing the hole then became clear: pull the hood through the hole so it would lie on top of the poncho in the direction of the flow of the rainwater.

Keeping the two corners from sliding together proved even

less of a challenge. I pulled the two Kelty toggles — red, spring released — off the pack drawstrings and ran them through the top rope to hold the grommets in place. Next I slid the ground cloth and back pad under the poncho.

I kept my waterproof pack cover on my pack, which I propped against a tree. Not long after I finished, a pickup truck filled with lumberjacks stopped at the bridge. I walked down from my campsite thinking they might have news of the others but they walked past me to fill their beer cans from the stream. As nonchalantly as I could, I told them I was looking for two hikers, one of whom left ahead of me and one behind, and asked if they heard of the "Old Logging Camp." One replied, "There's a lumber camp about a quarter mile down the Paper Road." "The *Old* logging camp," I said, "On the Appalachian Trail." He shrugged.

"You see, I don't know what to do. Should I stay here, go back and look for them, or keep walking?"

"You might as well stay here. You got your tent up already. Besides, you couldn't ask for a better view."

I ate some peanut butter on Logan Bread and read Cuckoo's Nest, in retrospect, maybe not the best book for someone on the brink of losing his sanity. I then ate another piece of Logan Bread. Darkness came and still my partner had not reached me. I was determined to rest, to get back my strength before I began searching. But was I avoiding my responsibility? If he's dead, he's dead; but what if he's not dead, what if he is two hours away from being dead and needs help now? I was shivering. I took my boots and wet socks off and slipped into my sleeping bag.

Maybe I could flag a passing jeep and get a ride to a telephone so I could call my dad; he would know what to do. My dad served in both WWII and Korea, with Officer Candidate School and law school jammed in between. Of course he is pretty old by now; he will turn fifty in October, but he is still reasonably sharp. He makes decisions all the time at work and at home; what decisions have I ever made? I needed his help. Should I go back, even if that means going all the way to Nahmakanta Lake, or should I sit here waiting for my partner to eventually show up? What if somehow he slipped by me and was waiting for me at the next lean-to? If that were the case and I went back, I would never find him; I would spend the rest of my life walking back and forth over the same fourteen point five miles while he sat with the silent hiker at the next lean-to.

Maybe Rand was testing me. On every day of this journey he passed me and then waited for me to show up to our destination. Maybe he zipped by me while I stooped to get water from the spring or maybe he deliberately failed to show to make me see what waiting feels like. I never purposefully finished late, and I think I walk fast, but he moves like a sled dog. I am an amateur walker to his professional hiker. I lay in the sleeping bag sucking on a tablespoon of peanut butter to warm my body. After a while, I fell asleep. All the while it rained.

Later, I can't tell how much, I awoke after hearing four whooping sounds. I sat up wondering "Could that be him?" The sounds were repeated. Maybe he is walking by, looking for me. It was pitch black out; I could not see a thing. "No. It couldn't be him," I reasoned as I lay my head back down, "the international distress signal is three, not four."

I awoke the next morning at first light, still alone. How could I have passed the blue tent? Did the silent hiker leave first? My father would know what to do. Maybe the new lumber camp would have a phone; I could call him from there. Maybe they would serve a hot breakfast. At the very least, I could see what a lumber camp looks like. I stuck a note on my pack and began walking in the direction the lumberjack had pointed. Where was my partner? If only I turned back sooner, he might still be alive. I had to find him.

As I walked upon the wide gravel road the lumber company built through the forest, I thought about last night. I recognized the pointlessness of searching in the dark. I also realized that calling my father would only worry him since there was nothing he could do from 800 miles away. No, I got myself into this and I needed to find my way out. A wave of desperation came over me again; I felt nauseous and chilled. This was far more serious than anything I ever faced, but it could be boiled down into two parts: the problem and the solution.

The simplicity of this structure relaxed me. I have a problem and now I just need a solution. I thought more about my father. When I was young and if the family faced a difficulty, my father never gave the appearance of panic. Whatever the problem, he moved deliberately, with calmness. I wondered which came first, the calmness or the appearance of calmness. I realized my longing for my father to take charge cast me in a lesser role, as a follower, and not a leader. I needed to look strong so I could be strong.

After twenty minutes of walking, I found no sign of a logging camp. Without a pack, I could walk four to five miles an hour so I covered a lot more than the half mile. Why did I have such trouble finding logging camps?

I returned to my pack, ate a quick breakfast of Logan Bread and peanut butter and then filled my pockets again with my emergency equipment and the rest of my share of the Logan

Bread. I figured the Old Lumber Camp must be somewhere between Mud Pond and Cooper Falls, but I vowed to walk all the way back to Nahmakanta Lake Lean-to if need be. Finally, a decision. What relief I felt. Resolved, I left for my search.

Free of my pack, I walked quickly, randomly blowing three notes on my whistle. I knew that the worst disaster would be my own death; that would definitely ruin the trip. But what if my partner were dead; would I finish the Trail? What would I tell his mother? What a great way to introduce myself. I passed through the area where the old lumber camp should have been. No sign of anybody. I looked left and right for a blue tent; I blew my whistle. I shouted for Rand.

I balanced myself over the sapling shakily bridging the outlet from Mud Pond. I crossed the mouth of the pond on its series of submerged logs: still no sign.

By replacing action for indecision, I shook the cobwebs in my brain. I knew I would find him, one way or the other. My decision gave me energy. I climbed the next hill — nothing. He must have broken his leg or hit his head against a rock. If injured, I would carry him to the Great Paper Road or fix him up in his tent, then go for help. By Mud Pond I concluded that only an injury could have kept him back but I would rescue him.

On I went. I would go all the way back to the lake; I would find him, regardless of his condition. I willed myself to be calm and then let the calm create my confidence. Yesterday, I was so tired and scared I could barely breathe. Today, I was certain I would find him.

From the beginning, I approached this trip with confidence. I assumed a lot — if only I could assume my partner were still okay. I shouted for him. I was nearing the Old Antler's Camp. How could he not reach the Old Antler's Camp after a day of hiking? I blew my whistle. I shouted his name. No answer. I ran. He must be dead, I thought — or worse.

Then I heard a dog bark.

I stopped running. There he was, that crazy malamute, standing in front of a red pack leaning against one of the dilapidated cabins. My partner, yawning sleepily, stepped out into the sun.

"Are you all right?" I said.

"I thought you said 'the Old Antler's Camp.'"

He was okay. Not a scratch on him. No broken bones. Nothing. I looked at his neck but it did not look broken. My mind, so filled with worry and fear, went blank.

"Get your pack on," I said slapping him on the back, "Let's go."

End of excerpt

The Long Green Tunnel is available on Amazon

ABOUT THE AUTHOR

David Barol is a husband, father, author, speaker, trainer, and financial consultant. He is an avid outdoorsman whose passion for hiking inspired the Notes from the Trail series: *The Long Green Tunnel* and *The Glorious Quest*.

David holds a B.A in Political and Social Thought from the University of Virginia, a Masters in Public Policy from Harvard University, and several professional certifications, including Certified Financial Planner (CFP), Certified Life Underwriter (CLU), and Chartered Financial Consultant (ChFC). He writes frequently on both public policy and financial matters, including the KeyAMS series on personal financial planning.

When not pursuing his day job, David spends his time with his family and community. You can find his books at www.balahousepublishing.com, on Kindle, or wherever great literature is sold.

www.ingramcontent.com/pod-product-compliance
Lightning Source LLC
Chambersburg PA
CBHW021052090426
42738CB00006B/300